THE AESTHETICS OF THE MIND
AFTER MALLARMÉ

THE AESTHETICS OF THE MIND AFTER MALLARMÉ

Aldo Trione

Problems in Contemporary Philosophy
Volume 36

The Edwin Mellen Press
Lewiston/Queenston/Lampeter

Library of Congress Cataloging-in-Publication Data

Trione, Aldo.
    [Estetica della mente, dopo Mallarmé. English]
    The aesthetics of the mind, after Mallarmé / Aldo Trione ;
translated from the Italian by Gordon Poole ; edited by Sergio
Sorrentino.
          p.   cm. -- (Problems in contemporary philosophy ; v. 36)
    Includes bibliographical references and index.
    ISBN 0-7734-8763-8 (hard)
    1. Aesthetics. 2. Aesthetics--Psychological aspects. 3. Poetics.
I. Sorrentino, Sergio. II. Title. III. Series.
BH39.T6713 1996
111'.85--dc21   96-46459
                                                                      CIP

This is volume 36 in the continuing series
Problems in Contemporary Philosophy
Volume 36 ISBN 0-7734-8763-8
PCP Series ISBN 0-88946-325-5

A CIP catalog record for this book is available from the British Library.

The Edwin Mellen Press   The Edwin Mellen Press
        Box 450   Box 67
Lewiston, New York   Queenston, Ontario
   USA 14092-0450   CANADA L0S 1L0

The Edwin Mellen Press, Ltd.
Lampeter, Dyfed, Wales
UNITED KINGDOM SA48 7DY

Printed in the United States of America

TABLE OF CONTENTS

PREFACE

L'exercice de la poésie laborieuse m'a accoutumé à considérer tout discours et toute écriture comme un état d'un travail qui peut presque toujours être repris, et modifié; et ce travail même comme ayant une valeur propre, généralement très supérieure à celle que le vulgaire attache seulement au produit:

thus wrote Valéry in a passage in the *Cahiers.*

The concept of *poésie laborieuse*, which among other things makes it possible to grasp some of the variations in the idea of *poiesis* in the aesthetics of the twentieth century, raises fundamental questions on the relationship between the *cogito* and art, on the nexus between poetry and temporality, on the notion of writing, combinatory play, figures, etc. Above all, it leads us *beyond* Mallarmé. Indeed, he questioned himself with disquieting modernity as to **what poetry is**, but his inquiry remained within the confines of **literature.**

On the contrary, Valéry, although moving within the aesthetic perspective suggested by the author of *Igitur*, took his stand decidedly against any sort of literary ideology. Through the making of poetry, he directed his inquiry into the hidden empire of the mind, its mechanisms and manoeuvres. In the footsteps of Valéry's reflection, this volume attempts to conduct its exploration in the intricate web of *poiesis* and its enigma.

Aldo Trione

Naples, June 1992

I

THE AESTHETICS OF THE MIND:
AFTER MALLARMÉ

1.   Literature, notes Valéry, is not my main concern: it interests me only as an example or attempt to say "ce qu'il est difficile de dire."[1] Such an idea of literature leads him to consider poetry as a space pertaining to abstract reflection which, however, does not satisfy exhaustively "all the passions of the mind nor its various functioning needs." The author of *Monsieur Teste* asserts that *poiesis*, understood in its widest sense, interests him only when it contributes to the growth of the mind itself. The works are nothing but an exercise, a play, an application or an act externe to be considered without reference to such categories as authorial presence, emotivity, inspiration. I would not have written my verses, he writes, had I not almost prevented their being made by the conditions I imposed on them and which "ne sont pas toutes visibles."[2] The works thus being activities capable of transforming things into a multiplicity of possible expressions, writing requires that particular data and manners be translated within a precise system of general definitions and that, finally, "cette transposition" be retranslated into ordinary language. One can therefore talk of "pure literature," which must be based on the least number

---

[1] C. (=*Cahiers*, vol. I, Paris 1973; vol. II, Paris 1974), I, p. 258.

[2] C., I, p. 261.

of direct stimuli from the person and on the most ample recourse "aux propriétés intrinsèques du language."[3]

In the great exploration of the mechanisms and the "hidden" logic of thinking conducted in the *Cahiers*, constantly redrawing the most arduous and complex motifs of his philosophy, Valéry almost obstinately "recovers" the salient features of his poetics. The fragments collected in the *Ego scriptor* section allow certain significant theoretical clusters, which still today appear of great moment in aesthetic reflection, to be grasped with exemplary clarity. It is sufficient to consider the problems related to the phenomenology of writing. Writing means setting a mental process into motion, constructing a hypothesis of calculation, imposing particular, very hard, conditions of existence on the work; in other words, before the practice of writing setting up in opposition the ensemble of the possibilities of modification, transformation and variation "qui définissent l'esprit même."[4] Only following this path can one understand certain "resolutions" of semantic and phonetic dissonances arranged on a plane situated above the ingenuous conceptions of literature. There is need for work of a combinatory kind, analogous to that performed by musicians working with the calculations of harmony. We seize upon the words and rearrange them in an order completely different from that of normal use. Literary works, therefore, require numerous prolegomena: "expositions, descriptions, preparations, the functions of which are, on the one hand, to define the components and the rules of the game, and on the other, to

---

[3]C.,I, p. 272.

[4]C.,I, p. 281.

familiarize the unknown reader with the author's sensitivity."[5] In fact, the conventions and the postulates are the data "starting from which the work itself can be understood."[6]

But how is the work constituted? What is the proper nature of *poiesis*? What does it reveal or conceal? Perhaps *poiesis* is only the place of unexpected sonorities or symmetries and improbable correspondences between form and range of meanings. Certainly, when a work is being made there is a first state where a word, a formula, an image and a device appear, which will subsequently be arranged in a composition, "to serve unexpectedly as a seed or as a solution . . . ," to be resolved finally in a "non-linear" manner in a stage that is never concluded or solidified, or separated from its chances and possibilities of transformation. *Poiesis* thus tends to disengage itself from the external and to set itself as an instrument of discovery, "like an algebra which now discovers its own properties," now grasps the relations between things, to which its letters "sont rapportées par des définitions et conventions physiques ou autres."[7] At such a stage the work stands on its own, by virtue of its structure, not on account of its resemblances with or its relation to the external, and still less on account of a direct link with the passions of life.

---

[5]The quotation is from *La création artistique*, a conference held on February 28, 1928 at the *Société française de philosophie* in ``Bulletin de la Société française de philosophie," January 1928, published in ``Vues," Paris 1948. It is a text not included in the *Oeuvres*. Vid. the Italian translation in the anthology Paul Valéry, *La caccia magica*, ed. M.T.Giaveri, Napoli 1985, p. 35.

[6]Ibid.

[7]C.I., p. 290.

Valéry talks of the *Enchantement* of making, determined in a *liaison* between heteroclite elements such that their "sympathies" justify their match as far as possible. It is a matter of a pure constructive sensitivity, starting from which the author of *Teste* decided to choose *le parti singulier* of attributing to the music and to the modulations and inflections nearly all of the *fonction d'enchantement*, preserving the ground of his thought – or expressing it only when he could not keep it in the wings of the poem – to direct "sans se montrer."[8] To "direct" here means not to take words for beings or partial effects for total causes; it means considering that in the *poiein* content, ideas and images are mere accidental products, subordinated to the figure of the form, which is the organic unity of the work; in other words, it is what makes the work a unity of passion and action and a moment of poetic universe, whose secret resides in the subordination of the immediate products of the mind to the conditions of the language "en tant qu'excitant probable."[9] To pursue the figure of the form requires one to pose the problem of transforming the emotional substance in a "compositional" register constructed under the sign of abstract laws and forms which, nevertheless, impose sadness, tenderness, regret, depth of memory. The "composition," however, must not reveal that one is burdened by chains. In short, the fulfillment of art consists in not losing any of the shades of fantasy, "cependant que l'on veille à l'exactitude de l'ordonnance et que l'on s'astreint à ne pas errer hors d'un programme des plus

---

[8]C.I., p. 309.

[9]C.I., p. 309.

sévères."[10] The *nuances de la rêverie* must not be associated with a vague and confused psychological idea of pleasure, which in the history of culture has acquired, as we know, an eminently functional role in the mechanism of the conservation of the individual.

Is it possible then to introduce into an intellectual construction, such as art is in fact, a *topos* as indistinct and imprecise as pleasure? Certainly, there is the pleasure that communicates the illusion we deeply understand the object producing it; such an object stimulates and challenges the intellect and is capable of presenting itself as a *source sans terme certain*. This pleasure, without a well-defined purpose and lacking a completeness that can be expressed in finite notions, is configured rather as an abstract desire to create for the sake of creation, characterized by enigma and mystery, for which the philosopher attempts to find a collocation and an intellective function. But faced with such a monster of the *Intellectual Fable*, in which are combined sensation and action, instinct and reflections, rhythm and limitlessness, the philosopher can only repropose his absolute logic and categories, i.e., his *Pure Notions*.

In pursuing this magnificent prey, he finds himself involved in a magic hunt. Thus it comes about that while poets lose themselves in the forest of Language, becoming inebriated with bewilderment, seeking crossroads of meaning and unexpected echoes, fearless of the meanders, surprises and darkness, the hunter (the philosopher) seeks the "truth" in these facts, following a single and continuous path. However, he does not catch anything

---

[10]O. (= *Oeuvres*, vol. I, Paris 1957; vol. II, Paris 1960), II, p. 1370.

at the end. Moreover, the application of dialectical analysis to problems not contained within a well-defined field cannot but produce "truths" within "l'enceinte conventionelle d'une doctrine."[11]

This is the reason why metaphysical aesthetics, which tends to replace the immediate and unique effect of phenomena and their specific resonance with intellectual knowledge, actually exempts us from experience of the Beautiful, as it manifests itself on the plane of sensibility. Furthermore, addressed as it is to fixing the essence of beauty in general formulae, this aesthetics ends by considering works only as examples or mere intellectual opportunities (although it will never admit to not needing the sensory, i.e., world and things), as fragments of a universal and definitive truth. Moreover, all metaphysics tends to pronounce final judgements on the "uncertain matters." But what is the universal, Valéry asks himself, if not a "particular" effect or a point of view, i.e., a *decision taken* (*parti pris*), so that every universe we form "répond à un point unique"? Only with this "non-universalistic" perspective is it possible to establish an aesthetics which is not abstractly metaphysical but strictly pure, "raisonnée," addressed to the comprehension of the goals of art – an aesthetics which pushes its own claims so far as to forbid certain means or to enjoin certain conditions regarding the fruition and the production of the works. It defines laws by which the numerous conventions can be ordered and from which "les décisions de détail qu'un ouvrage assemble et coordonne"[12] can be derived. These formulae, in

---

[11] O.,I, p. 1301.

[12] O.,I, p. 1305.

certain cases possessing "vertu créatrice," can suggest ideas, moving and stimulating manifold inventive and productive processes.

Having reconstructed the problem in these terms, Valéry introduces the concept of *parti pris* into his discourse, within which lies the key to his whole theoretical venture, i.e., to his exploration of the functioning and the mechanism of the mind. The idea of "parti pris" is a fundamentally subjective one, capable of bringing into question the very legitimacy of reason in its claim to unify things and resolve them on a logical-abstract plane. Reason – *auguste Raison* – is, in fact, a goddess whom we believe ever-vigilant, who often appears to us "to invite us to calculate the diverse probabilities of the consequences of our actions"; she advises us to simulate a "parfait égalité" of our judgements, a distribution of expectation free from "préférences secrètes," and in this implies *our absence*. In short, reason would want us to identify ourselves with the real, with the aim of dominating it. But what does this mean? Is there a split between us and things? Are we not *real*? Furthermore, if reason tends to *reduce* everything to the abstract laboratory of thought – tendencies, differences, inequalities, injustices – what is the sense of things? How is it possible to "reconcile" the variety of things with the "unifying logic" of thought? Artists' works, also as concerns the proper "mental" context of their labour, cannot be reduced to operations of "pensée directrice," since the material or the means and a considerable number of unforeseen events introduce the unexpected and the indeterminate into *poietic making*. Artistic creation, in fact, often renders itself even *rationally* inconceivable the more strongly it is situated within the horizon of things, where from something *thinkable* it turns into something *sensible*. That is why the *necessity* of the poet – who cannot detach himself from the "sentiment de l'arbitraire" – is different from that of the logician: "Elle est toute dans l'instant de ce contrast, et tient sa force des propriétés de cet instant de résolution, qu'il s'agira de retrouver ensuite, ou de transposer ou de prolonger, *secundum artem*."[13]

Whence it follows that if the *fundamental* feeling of the artist is that of the *arbitraire*, art is nothing but a combination of heteroclite elements, born from the need to complete or to *respond* with the "symmetric," to fill an empty time or bare space and to fulfill an expectation: the whole combines harmonically on the plane of the transformations that the intellect can perform, making use of procedures borrowed from experience. Such procedures allow the creative and productive faculty of the mind to achieve high degrees of necessity which, in their turn, are configured as a kind of "answer" to the variety and the indeterminacy of everything which, in us, is *possible* or contingent and arbitrary or ephemeral. This is what we call a "work of art." It is the "result" of an act the *finite* purpose of which is to provoke "développements *infinis*": the work is, thus, essentially *production of effects*. This requires, on the part of the artist, a rare equilibrium of his faculties, i.e., self-mastery, and the control of technical means, i.e., the capacity, during the work, to ask himself the *right questions*, in hopes of achieving both *an act* that aims at "precision" and a movement that tends towards *charme*. The former refers to a *present* model, the latter consults a "hidden truth." These two actions flow together into the creation of the poetic universe, where an *infinite*

---

[13]O.,I, p. 1307.

transformation of traditional terms or rules and a mixture of perfectly incoherent psychic or auditory stimuli are fulfilled; the poet works on the complicated material of language and *speculates* on the sound and the meaning of words, i.e., on their harmony; he works on the various arrangements of certain intellectual and aesthetic conditions and on conventional rules; he creates a *mechanism* which consists in the harmonic exchange between expression and impression, within a *horizon of making* which cannot be separated from the rigor of reasoning and of abstract thought, that is, of a *philosophy*, which does not reside in the "objects" of speculation so much as "dans l'acte même de la pensée et dans sa manoeuvre."[14]

In this perspective, literature, which is full of people who do not know exactly what to say, but "sont forts de leur besoin d'écrire,"[15] is *reduced to the essential of its active principle.*[16] It is worth specifying that this assertion is not entirely negative, if it is true that the *need to write without knowing what* is given here, Genette notes, for what it is: a force. It is an empty force, "which paradoxically contributes, and perhaps suffices, to *justify* literature."[17] In the idea of literature as a need of an indeterminate object lies the uttermost

---

[14]O.,I, p. 1336.

[15]O.,II, p. 575.

[16]Cf. G.GENETTE, *Figures*,I, Paris, 1966.(It. trans. F. Madonia, Torino 1969, p. 231).

[17]Ibid.

issue of Valery's aesthetics, which, as is known, has lived in the world of letters "as in a strange land," inhabiting writing "as if on a visit or in exile."[18]

Leading *poiesis* back, therefore, both to the idea of problem and to that of solution, and bringing back the specific context of literature to the combinatory work which makes possible the organization of the *universe of forms* (poetry is infinite work), Valéry places his rare and apparently sterile experience on an essentially anti-literary plane, which permits him to consider poetry as a *fact* and, ultimately, as a work of the mind. In this way he asserts, and underlines, the distance that separates him from the whole "history" of our literary civilization. While many (above all Mallarmé), Valéry notes in a passage in the *Cahiers*, ascribe to letters an "absolute" value – "c'est -à-dire valeur d'un but final"[19] – literature has value for me only in order to develop the expressive powers and the *pouvoir de construction*.

Valéry moves in the tracks of Mallarmé's theoretical project, which tended to isolate or lay bare and consecrate, i.e., to cherish and adore in secret, the abstract Idol of the perfect I – the idol which destroys all others and "donne au moins l'illusion de la plus entière généralité."[20] However, unlike his master who has preserved the word I, rigorously applying the *principle of negation or the exercise of power ensuing thereof,* Valéry attempts to attain a "pur et implacable" absolute, characterized by the same formal valency that governs

---

[18]Ibid.

[19]C.,I, p. 232.

[20]C.,I, p. 317.

algebraic operations and mathematical postulates.[21] Mallarmé lived in order to carry out admirable transformations in himself and to shift continuously from the imagination to the word, not conceiving any destiny for the universe but that of finally being *expressed*; Valéry has gone further, so far as radically to negate the very idea of art and to state that poiesis is the *material* of the possible operations of the intellect. So the meaning of Valéry's assertion emerges clearly: "I have nothing to do with literature." Here, then, is the mind facing the work, struggling against mobility, uneasiness, dissipation (in which, however, it finds incomparable resources). If on the one hand, in fact, instability and incoherence or inconsequence hinder the mind in its manoeuvres, on the other hand they constitute an extraordinary reserve of possibilities. That is why, if the general notions of art, literature and work are to be defined, there must first of all be an exploration of the vast field of intellectual production. Such an exploration cannot do otherwise than lead to the mind itself, to the pure play of reason.[22]

---

[21]"Les livres de mathématiques ne m'intéressent que parce qu'ils sont les seuls livres qui ont pour objet la manoeuvre de l'esprit'" (C.,I, p. 375); vid. the studies by J.DIEUDONNÉ, *La conception des mathématiques chez Valéry*, and by Y. BOUVERESSE, *Valéry, le langage et la logique, in Fonctions de l'esprit* (textes recueillis et présentés par J. Robinson Valéry, p. 183-191 and p. 233-235), Paris 1983.

[22]*Monsieur Teste* and *Agate* are the highest and most exemplary moments of this *poietics of the mind.*

2.   Questioning himself[23] on *poiesis* and its status or on the horizon of sense which it determines, Mallarmé defines verse (which he places beyond the *défaut des langues*) as *complément supérieur*. Verse, in its musicality, detaches itself from the reality of things; for it leads us, through *Transposition*, onto the plane of pure notions, which occur only when the quasi *disparition vibratoire* of every natural fact takes place. In the absence of the world, in that oblivion to which the poetic word confines every reference to things, verse reconstructs and reinvents from the ashes of many words a new incantatory and total *speech*, alien to language, after having denied with a sovereign stroke "le hasard demeuré aux termes." This speech produces a "neuve atmosphère" – the atmosphere of the infinite and of nothingness. We who, from birth, know all the exotic lies and the disenchantments of the world's turnings, writes Mallarmé, go *simplement* to the shores of the Ocean, where nothing remains but a pallid and confused line, to look at "ce qu'il y a au-delà de notre séjour ordinaire, c'est-à-dire l'infini et rien."[24] Beyond our ordinary sojourn, the poet annuls the world and replaces it with the *essence* of *poiesis*, *beauté*, in which the very strategies of communication are eliminated.[25] In *beauty* words are suspended in a sort of *vide de signification*, combining in a syntax whose structure is that of an "original Logic."

---

[23]V. *Crise de Vers* in OC, p. 360-368.

[24]The passage is from *La Dernière mode*, (OC = *Oeuvres complètes*, Paris 1979), p. 372.

[25]F. PISELLI has written, in *Mallarmé e l'estetica*, Milano 1969, "making poetry is cancelling the world and putting poetic being in its place; this is effected by placing a sheaf of silence between them, a heady moment when the sparks of beauty come together and shine."

In beauty words are exalted to the level of manifold "facets," the rarest and most valuable for the spirit, "centre de suspens vibratoire," which perceives them independently of their ordinary sequence: *mots* "projetés, en parois de grotte, tant que dure leur mobilité ou principe, étant ce qui ne se dit pas du discours: prompts tous, avant extinction, à une réciprocité de feux distante ou présentée de biais comme contingence."[26] In the timeless void of beauty, words become transparent; they acquire manifold meanings according to their "collocation"; they do not express "the thing," but allow one to "glimpse" the enigma and the enchantment hidden in the combining structure of letters and in the forest of syllables, in short, in those relations that constitute the foundation of literature and music. These lead to the threshold of Being, which offers itself to understanding and to listening through imperceptible and continuous transfigurations and correspondences. But the understanding of Being requires not so much a hermeneutics or a *poietics* as a *mysterious science* of the Word. What is the Word? Is it language, is it speech?

For Mallarmé it is a "principle" which develops through the negation of every principle. The Word turns into language which, in its turn, determines itself into speech and writing. Speech creates the *analogies* between things by means of the analogies of sounds; writing records the gestures of the Idea and preserves them. In the Word is the Event, is the very *poiesis* in the polyphony of its significations. The Word speaks and says things, names the world: it is absolute, infinite. In order to accede to its abode

---

[26]OC., p. 386.

Hyperbole is necessary, which releases us from the bonds of our paralyzed thought, incapable of arising and expanding: "Hyperbole! de ma memoire/ Triomphalement ne sais-tu/ Te lever aujourd'hui grimoire/ Dans un livre de fer vêtu. . . . " Hyperbole forms a sort of *epibolé*, which leads one to grasp immediately the idea in the objects, the eternal in the ephemeral, the duration in the transience of things.

The concept of hyperbole, however, has a double valence in Mallarmé (in which regard some of the remarks which emerge in *Prose pour des Esseintes* are significant): there is an ecstatic and an erudite hyperbole. The *excess* of ecstasy, which is openness towards the unpredictable future, is "succeeded" by the erudite hyperbole, which, as Poulet has written, not relying on an immediate impetus of being, "goes and seeks in the past the rite thanks to which it will be able, in the future, to expand again";[27] such erudite hyperbole is given as the recollecting point of *poiesis*. Both the former and the latter sort of hyperbole, however, delineate the horizon of the possible, the vague terrain of creating and imagining, of form understood as the place of pure virtuality. It is virtuality that is expressed in the *dance*, in its impersonality and incessant ubiquity.

Moving from the axiom according to which the dancer "*n'est pas une femme qui danse*," Mallarmé speaks of the dance as a metaphor, a figure of transformation, which suggest the idea of a poem, "degagé de tout appareil du scribe," as emblematic art that gathers in itself pure identity, fascinating being,

---

[27]G. POULET, *Les métamorphoses du cercle*, Paris 1961 (It. trans. G. Bogliolo, Milano 1971, p. 415).

far from empirical life since, face to face with it, the only imaginative "transport" possible consists in "patiently and passively questioning." That is why, if we will be able to lay, "avec soumission," the original flower of our *poetic* instinct at the feet of a dancer, then immediately we will discover, beyond the final veil, the nakedness of our concepts, which always remains.[28] The dance, in the atmosphere it creates (made out of nothingness) evokes limpid, scattered visions, giving back to us the sense of a rhythm that exalts the body and hides it; it leads us back to the deep sources of the Idea. Like poetry. The dance and the poem, in fact, take us near the absolute, in an incessant play of metamorphoses, of "trames imaginatives versées," in which consciousness brings us into close contact with being. Here the total "unreality," the "absolute fiction" is realized, "which expresses being when, having `consumed' and `corroded' all existing things and suspended all possible beings, it comes up against the ineradicable, irreducible residue."[29] What remains? Blanchot says: only the word *is*. "The word which sustains all words, which sustains them letting itself dissemble in them, which, even dissembled, is their presence and their reserve, but which, when they cease, presents itself . . . as a `flashing moment', a `dazzling flash'."[30]

This dazzling moment, that reveals itself in the gesture of the dance and in the "gushing" of the poem, is that in which "the work, in order to give being and existence to the `illusion' that `literature exists', asserts the exclusion of

---

[28]OC., p. 386.

[29]M. BLANCHOT, *L'espace littéraire*, Paris 1955 (It. trans. G. Zanobetti, Torino 1975 ? p. 31).

[30]Ibid.

everything, but, in this way, excludes itself; and the moment when 'every reality is dissolved' by the poem is also the one in which the poem dissolves and, made in the instant, unmakes itself in the instant."[31] *Self-dissolution* constitutes the *metaphysical reason* of *poiesis*. If Mallarmé "glimpses" and grasps, by analogies and illuminations, the sense of the decline of art, its silence or absence and nothingness, he knows that this decline is indissolubly engraved in man's destiny, in his "essential" ways; he knows that human reality is founded upon the word *is* and our rational and imaginary venture is made possible by it. Here, then, are the "states" and the "flashes" of poetry, which is considered total creation; here is poetry, understood as the *expression* of the Idea, brought back, by human language, to its essential rhythm – poetry that reveals the mysterious sense of aspects of existence and which confers authenticity to our sojourn in the world. Here, finally, are the words and the letters, which become symbols of the world, flowing together into a great, absolute Book: "tout, au monde, existe pour aboutir à un livre." The book, paradigmatic locus of *poiesis*, is freed from every subjectivist "inference" and expresses a hymn, i.e., the harmony and the joy, an utterly pure "whole" of universal relations: "L'homme chargé de voir divinement, en raison que le lien, à volonté, limpide, n'à d'expression qu'au parallélisme, devant son regard, de feuillets."[32] Expressing the letter in its totality, the book sets up a spacious play of correspondences, where a "solitaire tacite concert" is realized in which

---

[31]Ibid.

[32]OC., p. 378. In *Réponses à des enquêtes. Sur l'évolution littéraire*, the theme central to the book returns:`` . . . le monde est fait pour aboutir à un beau livre" (OC., p. 872).

the word, by the musicality that supports it, takes on profound and ever new meanings.

Thrown in the shipwreck, the dice (the reference here is to *Coup de Dés*) appear as the site of a possible "conjunction" between the void and the absolute, through "somptueuses" allegories which, if on the one hand, state the absence of objects, on the other reveal the strong and dramatic need of them. Following in the steps of the lesson of Fichte, Novalis and Friedrich Schlegel, transforming the Cartesian *cogito* in the self-evidence of writing, Mallarmé plans his own "total" work under the sign of the absolute renunciation of any residual subjectivity. Is this possible? In the terrible vision of a Pure Work, he has almost lost, as he wrote to Coppée, the capacity to understand the most familiar words. Nevertheless his thought has managed to think itself, having achieved a "mystical" conception of *poiesis* which has led him to dig into the abyss where consciousness, instead of losing itself, has found its solitude in a "desperate clarity." In this way, Mallarmé has been able to grasp the absolute in a play of absences, which requires a strict formal perfection, the creation of an "infinite" universe – an authentic *universe*. The written work "appears as if it had the weight, the mystery and the power of the world. It is as if it could not be. It withdraws from silence thanks to the extent and the number of the rejections which should condemn it to silence. It dominates the entire universe, being made by the dominion of words."[33]

---

[33]M.BLANCHOT, *Faux pas*, Paris 1975 (It. trans. E.Klersy Imberciadori, Milano 1976, p. 114).

The work, therefore, cherishes and reveals a Beauty which continuously displays and insinuates mysterious enchantments. Is not the "château de la pureté," on which is written the metaphysical adventure of *Igitur*, the location of this beauty? Mallarmé did not succeed in accomplishing the *Work* of his life; he only showed some fragments of it, in which, however, he "fixed" a system of beauties capable at the same time of the absolute and of appearing completely transparent to the mind which formed it."[34] In the impossibility of accomplishing the *Pure Work* Mallarmé illustrates his own failure, the *figure* of which is constituted in exemplary fashion by *Igitur*. The movement which governs this "fragment of fragments," wrote Blumenberg, is anti-Platonic: a descent from the absolute attempt to absolute renunciation. "In reference to the philosophical tradition, it is as if man, having freed himself from his chains, were to return into the depths of the cave not in order to free his companions from the shadows that blind them, but because he yearns to return to the shadow, having failed in the task of pure thought, of resoluteness before ideas. The book is the polar opposite of the idea. That is why there is again an apocalypse, in which a book is closed for the end decline of the line of the Elbenhon."[35] From this perspective, in fact, the book nullifies all differences, itself taking shape, in the indeterminacy of the present, as the "reality of history": the present arises only when the book is closed. "It is the only

---

[34]Ibid. p. 120.

[35]H.BLUMENBERG, *Die Lesbarkeit der Welt*, Frankfurt am Main, 1981, (It. trans. B.Argenton, ed. R.Bodei, Bologna 1981, p. 316).

absolute action possible. The end is the absolute."[36] But the place of the absolute is the realm of the shadow. "Tout était parfait; elle était la Nuit pure.[37] . . ." "La Nuit était bien en soi cette fois et sûre que tout ce qui était étranger à elle n'était que chimère."[38] Only in the realm of the absolute can the nascent thought assert itself, or, better still, can the problem of thought as impossibility be raised: "impossibility of thinking, *impossibility* as the root of thought itself";[39] and, finally, only in the realm of the absolute can the harmony "without words and without boundaries," which is established between the I and the world, be grasped. This is the sense in which Mallarmé, as Blanchot has noted, is alone in having drawn from consciousness and from the contemplation of words a supreme, complete ecstasy, and in having reawakened "that profound nocturnal assembly, not through verbal rapture and seduction, but thanks to a methodical arrangement of words, a singular and particular knowledge of movements and rhythms, a pure intellectual act, capable of creating everything yet expressing hardly anything."[40]

The *everything* is the *Notion* which is revealed in the spacious play of correspondences, in the errancy of the word; and it is set – outside any linguistic representation – in the non-place of analogy, situated at the threshold

---

[36]Ibid.

[37]O.C., p. 448.

[38]O.C., p. 448.

[39]Cf. J. Risset's *Introduction* to S. MALLARMÉ, *Poesia e Prosa* (ed. C.Ortesta, Milano 1982, p. IX).

[40]M.BLANCHOT, *Faux pas*, cit. (p. 124).

of metaphysics and the Logos. In *poiesis*, then, language is displayed in its essence: it founds a world and renders possible that authentic dialogue "which we are ourselves." Certainly it is also an "accidental means of expression,"[41] but it is above all "what exists in itself as an ensemble of sounds, cadences, and numbers and on account of which, by virtue of the concatenation of the forces which it represents, reveals itself as the foundation of things and of human reality."[42] Therefore, if the "rational signification" can do without words, outside of which it "ensures intelligibility and understanding between beings," "poetical signification" is a movement inside the word; it is what "is manifested in the fact and in the illusion that language has an essential reality, a fundamental mission: to found things in and with words."[43] The property of poetry is constituted in this movement, marked by symbols, analogies, enigmas, straining towards the absolute, towards the *impossible* realization of the Great Work, of which the partial works are only splinters recorded in the domain of absence.

Nothingness and chance, life and the absurd, intellectual combinations and the absolute, necessity and the Idea, the candle of being ("par quoi tout a été"), folly – these are the fragments of the universe of significations which Mallarmé has placed at the centre of his poetic interrogation, addressed to grasping and sounding the system of figures, images and consonances which

---

[41]Cf. A.PRETE, *Il demone dell'analogia. Da Leopardi a Valéry: studi di poetica*, Milano 1986; particularly, vid. p. 124ff.

[42]M.BLANCHOT, *Faux pas*, cit. (p. 124).

[43]Ibid.

"converge" in the *uniqueness* of *poiesis*. Such *uniqueness* is not only, Blanchot has observed, "what depends essentially on language but what recalls language to its essence and prevents it from being confused with its aims."[44] Thus, Mallarmé's reflection sets itself, for many reasons, beyond the very space of *poiesis*: investing the reason of thought and doing, it ultimately presents itself as a long, uninterrupted interrogation on the structure of the I and the original Speech, or on the absolute and absence, i.e., on the "logical" conditions of artistic creation and, above all, on the structure of the I, with which the interrogation on the absolute and forms is inseparably associated. Within this theoretical orientation, in which the work is considered devoid of any concrete determination, Mallarmé ultimately identifies thought with the abstract I – an I without emotions, motionless in its own functions. It is the I which "appears" in a disturbing scene in *Igitur*: When I reopened my eyes, I saw the phantasm of horror slowly absorb what remained of feeling and pain in the mirror and feed its horror on "des suprêmes frissons des chimères et de l'instabilité des tentures."[45] Here, finally, the mirror is rarefied "jusqu'à une pureté innouïe," until it separates from itself. In this extreme movement of

---

[44]Ibid. Blanchot's final observation: ``One might even believe that his work appeared to (Mallarmé) purified of all enigma, whithout the veil of the least obscurity would have led him to suppose one was penetrating in his poetry continuing to remain outside it, that one was considering from a non-poetic point of view, that one was comparing with the intent to challenge or to teach, using the means of discursive reason, an attitude unacceptable in itself, but which could only remain alien to the poet and appear to him as inconceivable. The accusation of obscurity which the critics have continued to level against him is only meaningful for the non poetical intelligence, or more precisely, if one imagines, putting forward a highly singular hypothesis, that Mallarmé's work does not pertain to poetry"

[45]Cf. OC., p. 441.

Mallarmé's thought there is not only, as Poulet has noted, a kind of "dénudation du Moi," but a "halt" to all vital development, to any sign of life, an "immobilization." The verse – "Il s'immobilise au songe froid de mépris"[46] – fully reveals the sense of the whole of Mallarmé's journey towards Absence,[47] towards that void that sometimes becomes "visible par la magie du language."[48]

3.   Renouncing the world means putting oneself in the condition of understanding it. Mallarmé, as few others, knew how to fulfil this precept. Aspiring to absolute delights, through a nearly ascetic practice, he refused every consolatory, easy solution of art. He achieved the discernment of its profundity, which is strictly contiguous with the profundity of our I. It was in this way, detaching himself from the common and vulgar vanities and illusions, that the author of *Igitur*, whose life – *infiniment simple* – was constantly devoted to the play of transformations, could conceive of no other destiny for the world than that of finally being *exprimé*. One could say, writes Valéry, "qu'il plaçait le Verbe, non pas au commencement, mais à la fin dernière de toutes choses."[49] The abode of poetry is in the Word, where it

---

[46]The thirteenth verse of the sonnet *La vierge*, OC., p. 68.

[47]Poulet writes: "La conscience de soi n'est plus une présence chaude de soi-même à soi-même, c'est la conscience de la place laissée vide par celui qui en se retirant a omis de déposer dans la glace son reflet" (G.POULET, *Entre moi et moi. Essais critiques sur la conscience de soi*, Paris 1977, p. 111).

[48]Ibid.

[49]O.,I, p. 622.

finds its supreme dignity. One need only think of *Coup de Dés*, where it is possible, for the first time, to see the figure of a thought collocated in our space. This work has the power to speak and think, and so to create temporal forms. Everything here becomes visible; silences materialize; instants emerge, penetrated by the idea that destroys itself in them. Everything renders itself tangible; nothingness has become sensible. The sensible has achieved such levels of rarefaction and significance as to reveal the naked essence, in immobility and silence. In this work, page by page, a spiritual storm moves to the limit of thought, "jusqu'à un point d'ineffable rupture."[50] And here a prodigy is achieved on paper: an infinite glow of the last stars quivers in the same "interconscient" void, where – as the material of a new species – the Word *co-exists*. The word and things as word, in a fixity without examples: *poiesis*. This "astral formation," ever new, charging itself with significance, displays the ideal spectacle of the *Création du Language*.

But what is the place and what the time of such a creation? Do categories such as place and time have meaning? To sound the forms of *poietic* invention requires a hermeneutics that allows us to grasp the infinite play of analogies in the nascent state. Mallarmé, who attempted an "emploi à nu de la pensée," sought to fix its design, making use of an *instrument spirituel* to express and "represent" the things of the intellect and the abstract imagination, so that his invention, which is born within the page intended as a visual unity, has been constructed in particular on the analysis of language, its text and music. In short, he has turned his attention to the problematic of

---

[50]O.,I, p. 624.

writing (the formation of words, the arrangement of letters), elaborating a *system* in which the page, addressing the glance that precedes and envelops the act of reading, must "command" the very movement of the composition; in other words, it must "faire pressentir, par une sorte d'intuition matérielle, par une harmonie préétablie entre nos divers modes de perception, ou entre les *différences de marche de nos sens*, – ce qui va se produire à l'intelligence."[51]

Thus, by introducing a *superficial* reading, strictly linked to a *linear reading*, into the hermeneutics of *poiesis*, Mallarmé, according to Valéry, has enriched literary theory with a *second dimension*, which has conferred on poetry a "new" ontological valence, committed to the page, the word and the text. This, indeed, is born from an *attempt* that originates in that moment in which it is conceived (it is "un mode de la conception"). Such an *attempt* is the "final" result of long exercise, experiments and an elaborate technical "capacity"; it cannot be reduced to the application of a visual harmony to a "mélodie intellectuelle préexistante," but requires rigorous self-possession, acquired through an "entraînement particulier," capable of guiding the complex unity of the distinct "parties de l'âme." It is along the lines of this attempt, finally, that Mallarmé's research takes on features quite different from those proper to "ordinary" literature (which pursues "particular" results and is therefore similar to an *arithmetic*); it seems like a kind of algebra, a *mathesis universalis*, which presupposes the "will to exhibit, to preserve through thought, and to develop the forms of language separately."

---

[51]O.,I, p. 627.

At the end of *Dernière visite à Mallarmé*, recalling a walk in the countryside during which the "artful" poet picked the *most ingenuous* flowers, lilies and poppies, Valéry "fixes," in a series of images, the sense of undifferentiated unity that Mallarmé's work reveals: they seem to dissolve in an incandescent space, in which nothing lasts but nothing ends; here it is as if destruction destroys itself "à peine accomplie"; here every difference between being and non-being is lost. The space of the undifferentiated is the place where the "supreme" play of the transformation of ideas is realized. Mallarmé's tending towards the absolute is grasped by Valéry, aside from the influence of Romanticism having its origin in certain intuitions of Schelling, within a metaphysical-linguistic course deriving from Leibniz (even though, we would stress, the author of *Monsieur Teste* had scarce knowledge of Leibniz's works and thought).

It is precisely in a context determined by Leibniz and Schelling that Valéry attempts, several times, a juxtaposition between the construction of an exact science and Mallarmé's project to refound the entire system of poetry by means of pure, distinct notions, completely isolated and removed from the confusion to which the multiplicity of the functions of language frequently gives rise in those who take an interest in artistic and literary problems. Within this horizon the author of *Igitur* has thought up and produced linguistic combinations far removed from those "clear" ones in daily use, often arriving at a sort of obscurity which is due to a rational practice and a need for abstraction that are analogous to the *forms* of science, in which logic, analogy and the consequentiality of the discourse lead to representations quite different from those we meet in our everyday life, until we reach *expressions* "qui passent délibérément notre pouvoir d'imaginer."[52]   It is an original, exceptionally audacious procedure (above all if one considers that Mallarmé had no knowledge of science nor any aptitude for it); it caused this great poet of the modern to wear himself out in an "effort merveilleusement solitaire" and to challenge the whole literary culture of his time.   Even though he never detached himself from the metaphysics and the mysticism which he "derived" from Villiers de l'Isle-Adam, Mallarmé did, nevertheless, know how to "graft" those distant *presences* (fantastic improvisations, meaningful gestures. . . .) onto the original system of his own ideas, succeeding in giving the art of writing a universal sense, *une valeur d'universe*, imagining that the supreme object of the world and "la justification de son existence" had to be a book.

The idea of the book, even though enveloped in something enigmatic, mysterious, hidden, *lives* in a multiplicity of crystalline systems and forms of perfection, where words are tied with words, verses with verses, movement with rhythm. The "whole" appears as a sort of "object," maintained by an intricate equilibrium of forces, far removed, by a marvel of reciprocal combinations, from "ces vagues velléités de retouche et de changements que l'esprit pendant ses lectures conçoit inconsciemment devant la plupart des textes."[53] It is thus that in the realization of his aesthetic project, meditating on every word, Mallarmé was able to take into consideration and catalogue every possible form, constructing a work that has seemed to *signify* itself to

---

[52]O.,I, p. 636.

[53]O.,I, p. 639.

infinity as within an *enceinte mentale*, from which nothing could emerge which had not lived a long time in the world of presentiments and harmonic arrangements, of perfect figures and their correspondences: "monde préparatoire où tout se heurte à tout, et dans lequel le hasard temporise, s'oriente, et se cristallise enfin sur un modèle."[54]

In the movement of this work (whose "fall," in time, seems almost determined "par une sorte d'accident") the essence of *poiesis* can be traced. In his "obscure" language, and within a consciously mystagogic perspective, Mallarmé has not defined the nature of this *movement* but has identified its sense, making use not of " systematic" procedures but of the illuminations and modes proper to every authentic "inner system" (which is decidedly different from both philosophical and mystical systems). It is a matter of "illuminations" of great moment and significance in the history of modern aesthetics. Mallarmé as interpreted by Valéry, has not only constructed the most original poetics of the nineteenth century (still in our own century it reveals itself to be very rich and extraordinarily fertile). He is, above all, the one who, as few others, resolutely posed the problem of the *proprium* of the work of art and its autonomous, self-sufficient significance.

What, then, is the significance of the work of art, what is its *essence*? Mallarmé's answer is unequivocal. The *Néant*, the impossible, i.e., deprivation, non-being and absence, constitute the *forms* of art. Art is determined in the making, in the word, which makes possible the birth of that event that we call the *work* – of course, the work which is wanted and sought

---

[54] O.,I, p. 640.

in the causality of intelligence, in an orderly way and through an obstinate analysis of conditions "defined and prescribed in advance." But even though the work eventually places itself on a transsubjective and meta-empirical plane, it cannot but affect the author, who, in some way, is forced to "reorganize" himself, that is, to rethink his relationship with making, with art itself. And to rethink the relationship with art means to reflect not so much on the finished work, its appearance and metamorphoses, as on the manner by which *poiesis* has been realized. Such reflection requires certain "atrocious" choices; the only ones which can permit us to *assert* the sense of art's tendency towards the absolute, towards extreme perfection.

In short, Mallarmé, the sterile, precious, obscure poet, but also the most lucid, the most perfect, the hardest on himself "de tous ceux qui ont tenue la plume,"[55] making refusals (which constitute the *conditions* on which literature attains ethics) and succeeding in identifying or "glimpsing" the sense of an *idée-somme* of the value and power of literature, has paved the way for Valéry to construct an original aesthetics of the mind. Thus the author of *Coup de Dés* has opened up extraordinary possibilities for poetic thought of the modern. His mysterious "tête" has weighed up all the conditions of an universal art, eliminated from poetry "les prestiges grossiers," erased particular ambitions, raising itself to the conception of a "principle" valid for every possible work; this "tête" has discovered, finally, that it possesses the capacity to dominate the universe of words. A capacity which is very similar to that of the great philosophers, who "se sont exercés à surmonter, par l'analyse et la

---

[55]O.,I, p. 642

construction combinées des *formes*, toutes les relations possibles de l'*univers des idées*, ou de celui des nombres et des grandeurs."[56] From the analysis (and also from the "reconstruction") of Mallarmé's formal and combinatory poetics Valéry moves to the construction of his "philosophy of art," in which, among other things, he attempts to resolve the conflict, latent in his nature, between a "penchant pour la poésie" and the "bizarre" need to satisfy his own inner exigencies. However, beyond the analogies and the consonances, the differences separating Valéry from Mallarmé are many. Such that the author of *Teste*, although accepting the anti-romantic intentions of the master, re-elaborates them *ab imis* and *re-signifies* them within a new theoretical "project," which, in its extreme results, arrives at the denial of the very being of literature and of art. Certainly, the "forme admirable" of Mallarmé's texts permits multiple, if not contradictory, interpretations, which require the reliable possession of very refined, philological and hermeneutical instruments. But the context of interpretation is nevertheless an "historical" one which, as such, does not allow us to get to the heart of the problem. That is why, for Valéry, reading Mallarmé, basically means initiating a theoretical "operation" of another kind, addressed to the construction, or rather, *re-construction*, of an anti-literary poetics, understood as a phenomenology of figures of transformation, in which the combinatory work of the spirit is associated with pleasure, and in which Syntax (which is calculation) is raised to the rank of Muse. The author of *Igitur*, in fact, pointed out precise "directions" which go beyond his own work. Meanwhile, although he

---

[56]Ibid.

preserved "literary" beauty in his poems, he addressed his art to "construction," so that, as he gradually progressed in his reflections, he was able to show, in what he produced, "la présence et le ferme dessein de la pensée abstraite."[57] *What he produced* is none other than a poetry that is "toute volue et réfléchie," whose movement has attained absolute levels analogous to those characteristic of the substance of music – poetry exempt from eloquence and narration, maxims and deep thoughts, free of certain human "failings" and facile locutions.

Mallarmé's poetry, on account of the "familiar" things it rejects and the *unexpected* it always manages to reveal, has produced a kind of harmony by virtue of which we can participate in a completely different world from the one in which words and actions correspond to each other; just as music constructs its *perfect system* in the world of noises (by opposing it), so Mallarmé's poetry has been able to grasp, through words, certain rare elements capable of realizing *unique* works, situated on the threshold of nothingness. Mallarmé, who, without doubt, is to be considered the *least* primitive of poets, founded modern poetry in the unusual, almost *hypnotic* juxtaposition of the words he used, rescuing it from suggestions of Romanticism, and restoring it to its original grounds. He has thus recovered the sense of the *magical formula*, discovered the value of the spell, which resides not in the meaning of the terms, but, rather, "dans leur sonorités et dans les singularités de leur forme."[58] The *obscurity*, the enigma of words, their *charme*, become, then, the modes of

---

[57] O.,I, p. 646.

[58] O.,I, p. 649.

being of *poiesis*, in whose movement, through "the mystery of language," "the mystery of things" has been represented. Poetry is set as the "enigma of the absolute." Since all is inexplicable (the *visions of the world* we elaborate presuppose certain dogmatic cognitive categories and aprioristically guaranteed "truths"); since our movements and actions are unintelligible; and since, finally, it is radically impossible to give complete, satisfactory answers to the questions of the spirit, nothing remains but the perpetual questioning of the enigma, precisely through the enigma. Mallarmé's work is inscribed in the path of this magical, remindful question, which goes far back into antiquity.

Valéry observes that, since poetry has links with some human condition preceding writing, every real poet still *drinks* at the fount of language and "invents" verses more or less in the way primitive men invented words. Consequently, returning to the source of language and the profound gesticulating of the origin requires a rigorous and controlled exercise of reason and strict mastery of manifold techniques and of sophisticated poetic strategies. This "return," furthermore, does not at all involve flight into the skies of fancy or the vagaries of *rêverie*. On the contrary, it requires an intense relationship with things, a voluntary and complete spiritual organization, that is manifested in the act in which the poetical event is fulfilled. Mallarmé has been "témoin" or "martyr" to an idea of perfection, under whose sign he has achieved a profound lucidity that leads one to suppose a system of thought inextricably connected with poetry, treated, practised and resumed "comme une oeuvre essentiellement infinie,"[59] the products of which are nothing but fragments, trials and preparatory studies.

In this light poetry is "la limite commune et impossible à atteindre" towards which all realized or realizable poetical works, in short, all the arts, aim. To reach this limit it was necessary for Mallarmé to become a *virtuoso* in the *discipline of purity*, and to bring into play the rarest elements of his intellect. Accurate, refined work, opportune corrections, continuous changes of course in the difficult navigation amidst words: all of this was necessary to transform the disorder of things into an intellectual, absolute order, which presented itself as the metaphysical seal of the making of poetry. Like those who "deduce" music from the sounds, Mallarmé has "extracted" from language, its modifications, its "tangible" and "historical" elements, certain prominent features have offered him some *projects* which were as unexpected as they were *realizable*; he succeeded, therefore, in fusing together poetic reflection or versifying thought, with the study of the relations that are set up within language, delineating a *theory of poiesis*, the complex problematical articulations of which it is not always easy to grasp. Moreover the problems an artist poses about the realization of a work insinuate infinite questions, require opportune choices and taxonomic methodologies. These form a veritable "science" of poetry which, although it has an individual value, tends, nonetheless, to set itself as a "model," as a theoretical system, as a doctrine of art. Creating the science of *his* words and investigating the figures of transformation of language, Mallarmé realized a space in which words

---

[59]O.,I, p. 653.

themselves were ordered according to the mysterious law of his "sensitivity."
Here, then, is the *âme* of this great protagonist of modern art, stretching
towards "les harmoniques," to "percevoir l'événement d'un mot dans l'univers
des mots, où elle se perd à saisir tout l'ordre des liaisons et des résonances
qu'une pensée anxieuse de naître invoque. . . ."[60]

The soul that searches the harmonies is the soul of the poet, who, in
attempting to take possession of the inner nexus of thought, rejects empirical
use of words and constantly creates a world of events in which the I and
Language end up by corresponding and abstract distinctions relative to the
relationship between form and content lose all meaning. In spite of the great
prominence which has been attributed to such distinctions by the aesthetics
and the philosophies of language, starting from the Romantic age, for Valéry
they are fundamentally surreptitious. In fact, if we turn our attention to what
we call *content*, that is, to isolated sensation and images of every kind, we
notice that we are faced by heterogeneous elements and impure forms, which
must be freed from their chaos in order to be represented in the "unifying
system of language," in order to constitute a *discourse*, in which the figures
become essential elements; the *inventio* is assumed as the very key to the
production of the intelligence, the *metaphor* takes on the value "d'une relation
symétrique fondamentale." In short, founding a "combinatory poetics" with
unequivocal ontological-hermeneutical traits, Mallarmé achieved a conscious
possession of the function of language and a feeling of a higher freedom,

---

[60]O.,I, p. 656.

before which "toute pensée n'est qu'un incident, un événement particulier."[61]
Only an extremely rare combination of practice and virtuosity with such a high
intelligence "pouvait conduire à ces profondes vues, si profondément
différentes des idées ou idoles que l'on se fait en général de la littérature. Il en
résulta que le culte et la contemplation du principe de toutes les oeuvres lui
rendirent sans doute de plus en plus pénible et de plus en plus rare l'exercice
même de l'art et l'usage de ses prodigieuses ressources d'exécution."[62] Valéry's
reading, it appears evident, takes us beyond Mallarmé; it introduces us to an
infinite exploration of the empire of reason in its worldless solitude.

4.   Mallarmé's verses, which are difficult to decipher and cannot always be
brought back to finished thoughts, cannot be interpreted on the plane of mere
literary signification. They are evidence or essences; their understanding
requires instruments more complex and informed than those proper to
"literary" knowledge. The approach to Mallarmé's poetic language is not easy.
At first, Valéry felt somewhat uneasy before those obscure, allusive verbal
constructions. Gradually, however, as he savored the rhythms, musicality and
scansion, the obscurities diminished and a precise horizon of comprehension
began to be outlined. And here, then, was disclosed the mystery beneath
certain strange combinations of words, beneath the extreme contraction of the
figures, the fusion of metaphors, the rapid transmutation of very compact

---

[61]O.,I, p. 660.

[62]O.,I, p. 659.

images "soumises à une sorte de discipline de densité."[63] The language of poetry, quite different, by its musicality, from the language of prose, emerged in all its purity. Thus Valéry, after the first difficulties in the approach to Mallarmé's work, came to deeply understand its value, uniqueness and unrepeatability; he grasped the surplus in it – the essence inherent to the structure of the spirit. Deliberately far from the images of everyday life, tending to avoid all realistic claims and at the same time all metaphysical preoccupations, Mallarmé's poetry has transformed existence into an universal event which succeeds, certainly, in moving or arousing emotions, but without "stimulating" ingenuousness or candour; on the contrary, it induces "les larmes et la joie les plus difficiles," those which, seeking their own cause, "ne la trouvent point dans l'expérience de la vie."[64]

Consider, in relation to this, an absolutely pure musical work, for example a composition by Bach, which, notes Valéry, never refers back to a feeling but builds a *feeling without a model*: in its high, uncontaminated substance the musical work reveals the idea of beauty, its value created out of nothingness, or, better said, out of the insignificance of things, and addressed to nothingness. It is in the universe of music that Mallarmé has placed his poetic work, organizing the words, forms and objects of prose in the order, precisely, of musicality and *pureté*. An order which expresses and "harvests" the utopia of *pure poetry* – an "order" set as limit, direction, *telos*. This was the great *project* to which Mallarmé attended all his life, from the time of his

---

[63]O.,I, p. 668.

[64]0.,I, p. 676.

youth when he used to frequent the Felibrist circles. Valéry quotes certain significant and revealing passages from the letters Mallarmé wrote to Aubanel. In one of these, dated 1864, the poet (then little more than twenty years old) speaks of the *centre* of himself, of threads that come out from his spirit which he clutches as a spider would do, of *meeting points*; and he extols his joy because he has been able to contemplate eternity within himself. In another letter, Mallarmé writes:

> Tout homme a un secret en lui, beaucoup meurent sans l'avoir trouvé et ne le trouvent pas parce que, morts, il n'existera plus, ni eux. Je suis mort et ressuscité avec la clef de pierreries de ma dernière cassette spirituelle; à moi maintenant de l'ouvrir en l'absence de toute impression empruntée, et son mystère s'émanera en un fort beau ciel.[65]

From these sentences emerges the design that was to mark the whole of Mallarmé's work – a work that was made possible by the firm decision to create starting from solitude, and, as it were, for the sake of solitude. Solitude that brings us back to *ourselves* – however, not to a psychologically determined *We*, but to the deep sources of being, where the I is *mingled* with the original language. From the "unity" of the I with Language can be *deduced* the poetry which says without being said, and which is *signified* in the great, only, Book of the world. Mallarmé did not go beyond these intentions. He pointed out a path. Is it possible to follow it to the very end? And where does this path lead? These are some of the questions Valéry posed himself when he wanted to interpret the *signs* of the poetic universe of the master, for

---

[65]The passage quoted is from 0.,I, p. 678.

whom syntax was an algebra which was to be cultivated in itself. Sometimes, Valéry recalls, Mallarmé used to like generalizing certain characteristics that syntax presents only in certain specific cases: either he would interweave numerous prepositions into a phrase, or he would venture into a sort of literary counterpoint that created *gaps* between words and ideas.

These subtle "constructions," which seem only to take place in the *context of the Letters*, reveal something more complex. They imply perspectives of great moment in the very strategy of knowing. In short, they help us reach "à la découverte de la structure de notre univers intellectuel."[66] In this sense, the book *Les mots anglais*, though so un-*philological* (it is in no way a treatise on the history of language or linguistics; it is nevertheless very rich in hermeneutical suggestions, possessing a productive and audacious cratilism addressed to grasping the essence of words), can, with full justification, be considered an exemplary document of the inner work undertaken by Mallarmé, who, in the nuances and even the minimal variations of language, has "fixed" the essence, *value* and significance of *poiesis*. He needed a long and patient rational exercise, through which he was able to submit to the "réfléchie" will the production of his whole work, which, in spite of the conditions and the "constrictions" that determine it, or perhaps precisely on account of these, has maintained intact its essential qualities, enchantments and grace. In this way, he raised the problem "de la volonté dans l'art" to the highest level of generality, attaining not metaphysical *inspiration*, but *illumination*, which revealed the essence of poetry itself.

---

[66]O.,I, p. 686.

Placing himself outside any humanistic tradition, Mallarmé has shown that the word (which does not show, does not describe, does not represent anything) can give birth to ideas, which are constituents of the world. Undoubtedly his is a mystical conception of language, which *becomes* an agent of spirituality, that is, "de transmutations directes de désirs et d'émotions en présences et puissances comme `reelles', sans intervention de moyens d'action physiquement adéquats."[67] Just like prayers, invocation and spells, which create the *things* they address. This *mystical* conception led Mallarmé to reflect deeply on the nature of art and to conceive the poetical work as the place in which values equivalent to the sonority and the physiognomy of words are produced. It is for this reason that rhymes, alliterations, figures, tropes and metaphors are not rhetorical modes of discourse here but substantial properties of the work.

Each verse *becomes* an entity, with its own reasons and its foundation. In it – in the continuous alterations of words and letters realized in the verse, in the play of correspondences, in the recovery of certain ritualism of mysteries proper to magical onomasiology, can be grasped a *code* analogous to that of hieroglyphics and symbolism, capable of unveiling ever new "significations." In this sense the orphic myth of the word, the quest for the *psefos*, the tension towards *pureté*, the sound effects, the dissimulation and the enchantment, can be considered the *prominent features* of Mallarmé's *poiesis*. These *prominent features*, if they have unequivocally *defined* the artistic practice of the author of *Igitur*, have strongly marked the birth of modern

---

[67]O.,I, p. 708.

poetry itself, within which horizon many poets, including distant and different ones, have expressed profound consonances and common aims. Suffice it to reflect on the extraordinary analogies between Mallarmé's conception of poetry and the problematics of Rimbaud's *alchimie du verbe*. For Mallarmé there must be "toujours énigme en poesie" (the *aim* of literature is "*d'évoquer les objets*"), therefore it is necessary to create a language that is ever new, musical and enchanting. Just as for Rimbaud, the task of poetry is to invent the colours of the vowels (black A, white E, red I, blue O, green U), to regulate the form and the movements of the consonants, realizing a *poetic word*, which, sooner or later, will become accessible "à tous les sens."

It is in the word, then, that Mallarmé and other poets contemporary with him have placed the *absolute*, and where Valéry grasps the truth value of poetry. Such truth is without the world and without history. Its law is Necessity. Outside the truth of poetry remains the world. But what is the *sense* of the world? What significance does its existence have? There is no other *excuse* for the existence of the world, notes Valéry, than that of offering the poet the opportunity to play a sublime game, lost from the start.

5.   In the idea of the book of the world, according to Mallarmé, lies the very *telos* of *poiesis*. This idea was born, as is known, in very ancient cultures, with the Jews and the Egyptians; it is alive in the Middle Ages; it emerges again between the Renaissance and the Baroque. In the Romantic age it "returns" in new forms. Novalis speaks of an *art of the Bible*, of the elevation to Biblical status of a Book which becomes "the model and real seed of all

books"[68] (elsewhere, however, Novalis observes that, in fact, the world of books is only the caricature of the real world, and that many books are no more than "fragmentary visions of the real world"[69]). At any rate, whether we move within the idea of a super-book which exhausts all the possibilities of language, or, albeit in a fragmentary way, we find the universe in a book,[70] we nevertheless always remain *inside* a *literary* vision of the world. Is it possible definitely to come out of the ideology of Literature? How? And with what results? This is what Valéry attempts, setting himself within a different theoretical perspective from that which informed Mallarmé's poetics.[71] Even if Mallarmé cultivated the abstract Idol of the perfect I, and in spite of the fact that the system presupposed in his *poietics* is something much deeper than a literary theory and consists in a secret "universalizing" tendency, Valéry maintains that within it, Poetry, that is, Literature, is nonetheless preserved. Mallarmé, in fact, did not concern himself with anything other than *form*.

The author of *Teste*, on the other hand, in penetrating the modes of making poetry (which he considers as *figures* of the strategy of reason) attempts to realize, in tiny fragments, an authentic phenomenology of the

---

[68]NOVALIS, *Werke*, Berlin – Leipzig – Wien 1908, (It.trans., *Opere*, ed.G.Cusatelli, Milano 1982, p. 274).

[69]Ibid., (p. 486).

[70]Cf. The pages G.R.Hocke devotes to the idea of the *Superbook* within the problematics of the *Ars Combinatoria* in *Manierismus in der Literatur*, Hamburg 1959 (It.trans. R.Zanasi, Milano 1965).

[71]On the relationship with and the differences with Mallarmé see Valéry's letter to A. Thibaudet in *Lettres á quelques-uns*, Paris 1952, pp. 96-100.

mind. This "difference" emerges significantly if one reflects on the distance between works such as *Hérodiade* or the *Aprés-midi d'un Faune* and the *Jeune Parque*. While Mallarmé's poems are made weaving on the form, with a subject whose pattern "n'est pas assujetti qu'à se faire reconnaître,"[72] the *Jeune Parque* does not have a subject but arises from the intention to define or designate "une connaisance de l'être," which it is not sufficient only to *recognize*. In other words, poetry, which constitutes the essential subject of Mallarmé's work, is, for Valéry, no more than one particular application of the powers of the mind, and serves only the ends of the expressive and constructive capacities of thought. In other words, through artistic doing Valéry wishes to act not so much on others as on the self, the I, for which only what contributes to increase the possession of precise acts and to exhaust possible generalities is of value: "Mon principe littéraire est antilittéraire,"[73] states Valéry in a passage from the *Cahiers*. And this "annotation" appears in many ways contiguous with the key thought of *Monsieur Teste*: "L'essentiel est contre la vie." Valéry, in short, maintains that literature (to which "des limites" are to be imposed) should be placed in parentheses where (and when) the adventure of the I begins; this I, precisely in the manifold and improbable variations which are constituted in the *poiesis*, achieves an *état d'enchantement*, an *état rare*, the products of which are exchanged only among themselves.

---

[72]C.,I, p. 297.

[73]C.,I, p. 286.

This perennial *exchange* of conceptual webs and relations determines the event – not literary, not tied to the excitation of the passions – which we call the *work*, and must *stand* on its own, "en vertu de sa structure." In Valéry, Mallarmé's "spellbinding" word, which led to ineffable regions of mystery and required mystical listening, turns into the site of a different kind of *Enchantment* – one that consists in the sensation of a relation between the elements or the idea-images, such that "leur 'sympathies' ou attractions mutuelles"[74] justify as much as possible their "rapprochements." It is in the web of this *liaison*, in which each element evokes others through contrast and similitude or symmetry, that poetry happens – this *discourse* in which the physical, the psychic, and the conventions of language combine their resources, endlessly. Thus in poetry, according to Valéry, it is not, as Mallarmé thought, Language that speaks, but *living* and *thinking* Being, which pushes the *self-consciousness* towards the "capture de sa sensibilité."[75]

Poetry becomes an itinerary of the mind, leading ever further, to a search with undefined possibilities of development and unlimited scope: *it turns into* "philosophy" which, however, is not to be understood as a doctrinal *corpus*, dedicated to the investigation of particular contents or knowing, but as an *art of thinking*, which "soit à la pensée naturelle ce que la gymnastique, la danse etc. sont à l'usage accidentel et spontané des membres et des forces"[76] – an art which tends to the increase of the potentiality of mind, to precision or

---

[74]C.,I, p. 291.

[75]C.,I, p. 293.

[76]C.,I, p. 361.

force and appropriate or fast reactions. Art is a "methodology of the intellect" which leads to not attributing any importance to the "immediate products," to the rejection of everything which is *fiction ignorant of itself,* to reconstructing, on the contrary, "fictions" and "values," to not seeking the *truth* but cultivating the forces and organizations which serve to seek or *make the truth*: "Et si elle est, elle sera trouvée."[77] In this perspective, art – which does not know the vague and the ephemeral but, rather, is able to "reconstruct" them – takes shape as a strategy founded completely on the intelligence, which, however, does not exclude the unconscious elements; indeed, it summons and then sends them away again, as necessary; it re-defines and re-distributes them on the plane of rationality.

The idea of art, finally, is associated by Valéry to that of literature (even though these two concepts are formally distinguished), whence it follows that every discourse which is concerned with *poiesis* in the truth of its forms cannot but refer also to the more general context of the *literary*, its institutional levels, its rhetorical and taxonomic modes and its "formative" processes. Leading the space of art and "literature" back onto common ground, the author of the *Cahiers* asserts that no artistic production has meaning until it enters into an "exercice supérieur de l'animal intellectuel";[78] and, in the same way, literature is charged with a positive valence only if it involves the use of all of man's functions, at their highest degree of clarity, subtlety and strength.

---

[77]C.,I, p. 330.

[78]C.,I, p. 340.

Literature should not generate other "illusions" beyond those which it produces and determines on entering into activity: "L'intelligence doit être présente; soit cachée, soit manifestée. Elle nage en tenant la poésie hors de l'eau."[79] It is precisely in the intelligence that the formal development "more mathematicorum" of the relationship accidentally offered by the senses and the emotions, is defined – a development taken to the extreme, in which the associations imposed by facts, i.e., the primitive notions, do not remain intact or *still*, but change by virtue of the hidden work that is performed in the subject. Thus there is no philosophy "qui soit au-dessus de la manoeuvre la plus générale de la pensée."[80] Everything must be led back to thought, to the mind forever playing its intellectual game. That this game, moreover, has been lost from the start, is of little importance. However one must always find out the stakes and the rules of this game of the mind:

> Un jeu est chose admirable à réfléchir. Il y a un objet, but, gain – de prix variable. Il y a des règles – c'est-à-dire des actes à faire, d'autre défendus, d'autres à ne pas faire sans risque. Il y a des données initiales, cartes reçues, premier à jouer, et l'adversaire – et le partenaire. Le jeu est donc un type que je me plais à voir dans sa généralité et qui depuis la guerre jusqu'aux arts et aux sciences et à l'amour et aux affaires est la figure la plus générale de l'activité – même des cultivateurs. C'est le type de combinaison du hasard avec les données, l'orientation, la volonté, la subtilité, le calcul. Tout est dans ce type, géométrie comprise et sort de l'homme."[81]

---

[79]C.,I, p. 340.

[80]C.,I, p. 348.

[81]C.,I, pp. 348-49.

In the game it is possible to imagine a "philosophy" as the art of thinking, independently from what one thinks – a philosophy which knows how to transfer abstraction, transformations and distinctions onto the terrain of that "synthesis of man" that is constituted by the mind. Philosophy, then, is more than a habit or will to manoeuvre thought and invention, which, passing through the particular senses, can lead us to the skies of being. It is a *technique* that leads us to examine the multiplicity of the conventions and meanings that "accompany" human realizations; but it also enables us to "glimpse" some of the courses of the *possible*, beyond the limits of the existent, beyond the space where the word resounds. When it tends to *acquire depth*, i.e., to place itself outside *mutable things*, thought ultimately detaches itself from conventional language, especially *from previously experienced states*, and *repetition*. In the skies of being we attain the *mental life* ("qui ne se répète jamais") where the cognitive activity is suitable to a "penser le plus loin possible de l'automatisme verbal"[82] – to a thinking which thinks *pureté* without *any need* of language.

"Philosophy" (even though it lives fundamentally *in* the philosophical word) has always operated to render language a more subtle, certain means of knowledge; in this sense (in its metalinguistic *tension*) it is to be "recovered" as the site of Form, and attitude or expectation.[83] In this sphere, however, philosophy is no longer the paradigmatic context of logical and gnoseological systems but the territory of intellectual manoeuvres through which somebody,

---

[82]O.,I, p. 1263.

[83]Cf. what Valéry writes in "Tel Quel," O.,II, p. 662.

at some time, thinks his life and lives his thought "dans une sorte d'équivalence, ou d'état réversible, entre l' *être* et le *connaître*, essayant de suspendre toute expression conventionelle pendant qu'il pressent que s'ordonne et va s'éclairer une combinaison, beaucoup plus précieuse que les autres, du réel qu'il se sent offrir et de celui qu'il peut recevoir."[84] This is why *theorein* must be considered "une affaire de forme," since, precisely in the elaboration of a form, Gaède has noted, "trouvent à s'exercer toutes les vertus et toutes les espérances de l'esprit. . . ."[85] That is why thinking, if it means "perdre le fil," also (and above all) means building *ad infinitum*, not in order to escape into the solitary regions of the imaginary but to *adhere* to the rhythms and cycles of the earth according to the nature of things.

To Tityre, who, in the *Dialogue de l'arbre*, asks: "Mais toi, penses-tu mieux saisir la nature des choses?," Lucretius answers: "Je tente d'imiter le mode indivisible . . . ô Tityre, je crois que dans notre substance se trouve à peu de profondeur la même puissance qui produit mêmement toute vie. Tout ce qui naît dans l'âme est la nature même. . . . "[86] In this way the problematics of the relationship between poetry and philosophy is defined in the context of a complex cosmological vision. Tityre *sings* the tree which Lucretius thinks. The tree inspires love in the former; it is an object of knowledge to the latter. Lucretius identifies the secret contact of the tree with the underground or nothingness and pain. Tityre, on the other hand, sees the

---

[84]O.,I, p. 1264.

[85]E.GAÉDE, *Nietzsche et Valéry.Essai sur la comedie de l'esprit*, Paris 1962, p. 302.

[86]O.,II, p. 187.

tree as the symbol of love, whose life is in pain and weeping. However there is a deep consonance in this "distance." Tityre *feels* what Lucretius interprets. Poetry resolves itself in thought.

"Love," Paci has written, "is life which, like the tree, sinks its fleshy roots into the soul; it is light which feeds on darkness. Rising into the sky, at the same time it immerses itself into the earth, where the obscure and ineffable fount of weeping resides, the fount that seeks expression, because weeping is what does not manage to express itself. Lucretius thinks . . . of the idea of plant, but it will be precisely his thought that will see as truth what Tityre feels as love."[87] The relationship that is established between *être* and *connaître* "speaks" the infinite adventure of poetizing thought, which reveals itself as *form*.

But is *form* the *ultimate* reality? If it is not so yet, is it possible that it might be? Or is *not-yet-being-so* a limit beyond which thought cannot reach? In the idea of form the very destiny of a philosophy is at stake, which has always sought to guarantee itself against the danger of *appearing to pursue a purely verbal aim* – of a philosophy in which, in any case, language does not at all define the *ultimate form* of reality and being, rather, a movement or a path, an event or an *energy*, which orientates the spirit. It is of little import if this *energy* is called "method" or "self-edification" or "increase of power."[88] Doing, producing, in brief, *art*, as a manoeuvre of the mind has no other

---

[87]E.PACI, *Introduzione* to *Eupalinos*, preceded by *L'anima e la danza* and followed by *Dialogo dell'albero* (It.trans. V.Sereni), Milano 1947, p. 27.

[88]Cf. E.GAEDE,*Nietzsche et Valéry* cit., pp. 303-04.

meaning apart from an *attempt* addressed to initiate a "general reform of thought," in which the idea of reason comes to be re-invented *ab imis*, sounding the depths of the I or nothingness. Such an idea, revealing itself in a multiplicity of figures, without reference to anything but itself, permits one to grasp, in their nascent state, the primary conditions of intelligibility, the living unity of the spirit. In such a perspective aesthetics is nothing else but the "philosophy" of this idea; it is the art of being and knowing. It is the story of the adventure of thought[89] in its drawing itself up towards the improbable space of expectation.

6.   In *poiesis* every movement consummates an *undefinable* alliance of the sensible with the significant – an alliance that is determined starting from purely formal conditions, which are gradually defined until they propose, or even *impose*, a "subject" or a nucleus of "subjects." In the poetic universe (where the particular is essential and where prediction, "la plus belle et la plus savante," is composed of the incertitude of discoveries) the intellectual modes have a function quite different than the ideas that "sustain" prose. What, then, is this *function*? What is its ontological-hermeneutical valence within the strategy of reason? Why is *poiesis*, in the multivocality of its references, to be considered one of the privileged grounds of thought in its being made?

First of all, *poiesis* is no more than a manoeuvre of transformation in which sensible, affective and abstract elements are distributed that "suggest"

---

[89]Cf.O.,II, p. 66.

the meditation of a "certain moi,"[90] which does not have the features of Fichtian selfhood, does not "found" the structure of the person, but is given essentially as the mobile, continuous web of relationships. In the second place, *poiesis*, the work of the intellect (and, therefore, not to be associated with the multiplicity of objects, which do not bear any particular relation to the mind), does not exist other than in *operation*. It follows from this that a poetical text ceases to be a *work of the intellect*, if (and when) it is used as a collection of grammatical difficulties or examples, "puisque l'usage qu'on en fait est entièrement étranger aux conditions de sa génération, et qu'on lui refuse d'autre part la valeur de consommation qui donne un sens à cet ouvrage."[91] A poem, therefore, despite the fact that it can be enjoyed and used on the terrain of the *history of culture* and of *documents*, is none other than a *discourse* that requires an inseparable relation between the "*voix qui est*" and the "*voix qui vient*" and "*qui doit venir*" – a discourse dedicated to sounding the deep sources of the mind.

The mind, which appears to seek to impose on its *work* certain characteristics completely opposite to its own, wishes, in *poiesis*, to withdraw from the instability and incoherence or incongruence that are the structural co-ordinates of its state. Thus, it acts against the interventions to which it is often subject; it reabsorbs the infinite variety of accidents, repels "les substitutions quelconques d'images, de sensations, d'impulsions et d'idées qui traversent les

---

[90]O.,I, p. 1505.

[91]O.,I, p. 1349.

autres idées,"[92] it struggles against that which it is compelled to admit and produce, against its own nature and "son activité accidentelle et instantanée."[93] In the production of the work, however, *dispersion* has an "essential" rôle: even though instability and incoherence, or mobility, dissipation and non-consequentiality hinder and limit the mind in its "constructive" and "synthetic" processes, they are, nevertheless, treasure-stores of possibilities, rich in extraordinary reserves, from which anything can be expected, such as unforeseen solutions, *charme*, images, signals and unexpected revelations.

In its penumbra, in fact, the mind can "pressentir" the truth or a sought decision, which are often at the mercy of a "rien." What we wish, sometimes, to conjure up (a memory, a sliver of a memory, a combination of words), is for us like an "objet précieux," to be held or to be touched through a veil covering it and hiding it from our eyes: the slightest accident is sufficient for it to be unveiled to us. Sometimes, Valéry notes, we invoke this "objet," which "devrait être," having defined it on the basis of precise conditions; we seek it after we are faced with a vague collection of elements, none of which looks likely to approximate to our need. "Nous implorons de notre esprit une manifestation d'inégalité. Nous nous présentons notre désir comme l'on oppose un aimant à la confusion d'une poudre composée, de laquelle un grain de fer se démêlera tout à coup."[94] There are (or so it seems) mysterious relationships between the *desire* and the *event*, between beauty, the order we

---

[92]O.,I, p. 1351.

[93]O.,I, p. 1351.

[94]O.,I, pp. 1352-53.

invoke, and *l'attente*. In these relationships even what appears arranged or fixed is continuously subjected to *deconstructive* processes which reveal to what degree the power of the intellect acts against itself and its own works.

Consequently, we can act directly not on the contents of our thought, but only on the freedom of the system of our intellect, in the sense that it is certainly possible to lower the level of this freedom, but, in order to have the substitutions and the changes we wish to be produced, we have to *wait: "Nous n'avons aucun moyen d'atteindre exactement en nous ce que nous souhaitons en obtenir."*[95] While we are waiting, certain desired solutions are revealed – the *productions* of works. But in their being made, the works (all of them) obey the same "reason," in their constitution they are *without differences*. The mind, when it realizes a work, scientific or literary, is subject to tensions such as gropings, lights and shadows, trials, improvisations and new starts. In other words, artists and scientists all identify themselves "dans le détail de cette vie éntrange de la pensée."[96] The work of art, however, has a particular valence, i.e., *l'aliment* and *l'excitant*; it reawakens within us the thirst and the source. In exchange for the freedom we give up we receive the feeling of "une sorte délicieuse de connaissance immédiate."[97] We entrust the work with the destiny of our reason; in it we free ourselves from the ties of subjectivity; it is here that we find the illusion of acting and expressing, discovering or inquiring and resolving or winning. This illusion has no moral or subjectivist valence

---

[95]O.,I, p. 1353.

[96]O.,I, 1355.

[97]O.,I, p. 1335.

whatsoever. Quite the contrary. In *illusion* the subject sets itself on a super-human plane; the strategic points which command intellectual life enter into action; the various conditions of understanding are organized within a new order. They are the musical and verbal, rational and significant or suggestive *conditions* that require a link between rhythm and syntax, a necessary relation between the *sound* and the *sense*, in which, through procedures analogous to those that preside over the world of numbers, certain convergences and correspondences are determined that only poets, "de temps à l'autre," are able to resolve.

In the context of these convergences, in the exploration of the immense field of doing and producing, in the complex morphology of *poiesis*, the activity of the mind comes in contact with the undefinable. In this way an "action volontaire" (which requires long research, abstract attention and extremely precise knowing) adapts itself, "dans l'opération de l'art à un état de l'être qui est tout à fait irréducible en soi, à une expression finie, qui ne se rapporte à aucun object localisable."[98] In this *adaptation*, in the combination of heteroclyte, distant states, the work *appears* an event or an act in which a "miraculous escape" is achieved from the world of the possible and an entrance into the world of fact; it reveals itself, finally, as the ultimate determination of an inexpressible state in finite terms. The poetic fact then becomes the infinite site of the world – the place which, in *determining itself*, "opens" ever new indeterminacies, implies the unpredictable and enables us to grasp the unexpected.

---

[98]O.,I, p. 1357.

7.   Writing for others requires a conscious renunciation of the rigour of the intellect, the depths of which are difficult to communicate. But *writing for writing sake*, that is, bringing our I to the apex of the desire to possess itself, to reach the end of its thought – which can be reached only by virtue of an "abyss of inner sovereignty" – means developing to the extreme the dynamism of the mind and the inventive faculties. This writing has no memory of events; *it does not recount*; it is not turned towards life. It exhibits certain "pure ways," which do not "receive" their being from observable reality; it does not have referents in things; it is not marked by chronological reasons; it offers itself, or, better said, it *signifies itself*, as the "presence of a collection of possibilities." The writing of *poiesis*, even though it appears to be "organized" for others, tends to pure play and nothingness. But what is the nothingness of writing? Is it the absence of words? Or, rather, is it the absence of the world?

In certain revealing pages,[99] Valéry writes that only in the sign of the idea of composition and construction was he able to conceive the drama of the genesis of the work. In this drama one can read, in an exemplary fashion, the *impotence* of poets (even the greatest) when faced by the problem of the "complete organization" of the poem, which cannot be reduced to a certain order of ideas or a certain movement, but is something much more complex and *significant*. If this is true, then it is suitable to deem the majority of works of art (even the most beautiful ones) "badly structured monuments," composed

---

[99]Cf.O.,I, p. 1438:"Il me souvient que l'idée seule de composition ou de construction m'enivrait, et que je n'imaginais pas d'oeuvre plus admirable que le drame de la génération d'une oeuvre, quand elle excite et déploie toutes les fonctions supérieures dont nous pouvons disposer."

of marvellous fragments but lacking organic coherence, devoid of the "wholeness" that is the fundamental object of every authentic poetic of the mind. The *wholeness* is not a metaphysically guaranteed totality; it is the *complete action* of the mind (which can be realized in *poiesis*) capable of allowing the feeling of the full possession of the contrasting powers within us: transcendent reasons, evaluations "sans cause," unexpected interventions, unforeseen illuminations; allowing the feeling, in conclusion, of

> tout ce par quoi nous sommes à nous-mêmes des foyers de surprises, des sources de problèmes spontanés, de demandes sans réponses, ou de réponses sans demandes: tout ce qui fait nos espoirs `créateurs' aussi bien que nos craintes, nos sommeils peuplés de combinaisons très rares et qui ne peuvent se produire en nous qu'en notre absence. . . . D'autre part, notre vertu `logique,' notre sens de la conservation des conventions et des relations, qui procède sans omettre nul degré de son opération, nul moment de la transformation, qui se développe d'équilibre en équilibre; et enfin, notre volonté de coordonner, de prévoir par le raisonnement les propriétés du système que nous avons le dessein de construire – tout le `rationnel.'[100]

The *complete action* is not only the object but constitutes the very *telos* of the aesthetics of the mind. It is an *action* that is difficult but *possible* to realize. When it is *achieved*, it lives a life of its own: it produces an enchantment almost inhuman that does not admit confusion of values nor an ordinary and composite vision of things, nor, finally, the "désordre monotone" of *externalism*. In the enchantment the syllables and images, the similes or contrasts and forms and the terms that are suitable to poetry are arranged autonomously, forming an "object" with a consistency of its own, distinct from its author. If the intellect, as such, admits everything and emits everything, art

---

[100]O.,I, p. 1484.

opposes it through "recoveries" it can accumulate outside itself and set within the boundaries of its *being made.*

Does the territory of art, then, become the place where the intellect is checkmated? Or, rather, does the opposition of *poiesis* to the mind constitute a sort of necessary obstacle, which reason poses in order to assert itself – a manoeuvre by virtue of which the I is *better able to determine itself* in the infinite web of its adventures? The reference, here, is to the idea of the I-limit, i.e the I which wants itself inasmuch as it *wants itself* – precisely in opposing its own productions – as the site of all transformations. Art, on that account, within this *poietics*, is no more than a "means" by which the I transforms a question that is only its own. The I which *can do* everything but needs nothing – and which could do without creating or producing. But the I, which could remain *motionless* in its self-reflection, does *something* anyway; *it* sets *itself* an aim which, however, is not outside itself, even though it arrays itself on the plane of appearance.

Art is one of the "aims" of the I, nothing else. To use an "argument" of Teste's, one could say that the I creates some beings (viz. art) that resemble it. It gives them eyes and reason and a "vague suspicion" of its existence. But the beings (the realities produced by the manoeuvres of the mind), in order to assert their existence, are led to the negation of the existence of the I. Their "eyes" see an infinite number of things, but they find it difficult to *recognize* the mind that realized them. In Teste's argument lies the key to understanding the sense of the relations which are set up between the alterity of *poiesis* and the selfhood of an I that tends, in the artistic artifice, to see and to perceive itself at "forbidden angles." But Teste's apophthegms allow us above all to explore the proper quality of poetic making, which is a work without a name or a subject – without an *ultimate* aim. Through this "work," which is fundamentally turned against life, the I, in order to achieve the perfection of form, must forbid itself the use of any word to which a *finite*, conscious meaning cannot be attributed; it must never use words which, in the penumbra of language, can find indistinct resonances and concordances.

Poiein thus means performing a natural work, which consists in a sort of perpetual, instinctive preparation – like the work of the ant – oriented in the direction of a *growth of consciousness*, pursued with obstinacy and constant instinct,[101] through exercises of the imagination and thanks to the possession of the instruments of forms and of transformations. In this strategy art is a "gait," a rhythm in the *making* of which the growth of the powers of the mind is registered. To the extreme limit. But what is this limit?

On the imaginary island of Xiphos there is an – absolute – *Tête trachée* which manages to look at things as they are, the pure Present, without "nulle signification," without high or low, without symmetries or figures: "ni passé ni futur – point de nombres."[102] In the dimension in which the Head (*Teste*) of Xiphos lives it is possible to grasp this variant of the concept of *cogito*: "I am not, I think." Which is equivalent, Gaède has noted, to "I do not think, I am," which, in its turn, is equivalent to "I do not think, I am not."[103] Absence

---

[101]Cf. C.,I, p. 173.

[102]O.,II, p. 442.

[103]E.GAEDE, *Nietzsche et Valéry* cit., p. 280.

constitutes the limit of reason, which, in its obsessive and incessant self-questioning, ends by exiling itself to the "nocturnal empire of nothingness." Thought thus postulates its own non-existence as a necessary attribute of perfection.[104]

In this way the lines of a *poietics* are traced that is decidedly nihilistic and can consent to the construction of an anti-literary and anti-humanistic *aesthetics of the mind*, and whose real field is the "reality of discourse," that is, words and forms.[105] This aesthetics, moving from the awareness of the non-essentiality of artistic productions as such, attempts to discover the "more general" rules of doing, in order, certainly, to dominate "extant literature, already written, and all the possible literatures not yet realized,"[106] but above all to explore hidden realms, discover relations and, ultimately, live the adventure of nothingness.

---

[104]Cf.Ibid.

[105]G.GENETTE, *Figures*, I, cit., p. 237.

[106]Ibid.

II

POETRY WITHOUT SOUL

1.   Novalis is right when he states that cold intellect is more capable of arriving at daring revelations than fantasy is, which often leads only to "the realm of ghosts." In fact, *Poiesis*, although it sometimes seems to dwell in the erratic courses of the imaginary, fulfils itself by *signifying* itself in extremely subtle intellectual relations and webs and within particular cognitive strategies. At its highest levels, in its "last stage," it *detaches* itself, separating from the person who set it into motion. The artist, therefore, cannot but become aware of the fact that the work (which is supposed to have become entirely *his*) does not belong to him, because, by this point, it lives a life of its own. The attention, so sharp and felt, of such a "romantic" philosopher as Novalis to the "reasons" of *poiesis* offers us the key to a problematical reflection on what we could call an "aesthetics of the mind."   This definition can certainly be aptly referred to significant moments in the artistic culture of the twentieth century; but it also grasps the sense of certain great "trends" in the overall history of modern art.   It is sufficient to think of the Baroque or certain extreme experiences of Mannerism.

The definition is especially suited to the Baroque, its improvisational and transitory character, the technique of *suspension* and unfulfillment, its expressive and communicative processes, its excessive or "over-abundant" and metaphorical, analogical, often obscure or mysterious and initiatory language, which, at the same time, is rigorously inscribed in the dimension of the ingenious control of the mind.

In short, in the restless, polyvalent and artificial baroque word, a poetics of artifice is defined that brings particular techniques into play addressed to fostering rare subtlety and wit and producing determined effects. It is in this way that the word (and here we are referring especially to the experience of Cultism), while it *is laden* with multiple, improbable meanings, paradoxically narrates the slow agony of things and their fundamental insignificance. Any reference to the world seems almost to dissolve in the mystery of the analogy and in the artificial beauty of the *conceptuar*, i.e., in that act of *intendimiento*, which does not "fix" things in a cognitive theoretical scheme but presents itself through the *correspondence* determined between objects. These "disappear" in the play of infinite metaphors, which allow one to glimpse heterogeneous transitions and blends; they disappear, finally, in the labyrinths, alliterations and symbols which, if they appear to be modes of a frozen, laborious nothingness, are not at all *figures* of that *vain* herbarium of metaphors and witticisms which Borges[1] speaks of in relation to Graciàn; on the contrary, they constitute the conditions of the *being-there* of *poiesis*, which *is made* under the sign of the astuteness of reason and the calculation of writing.

In this perspective the   syntactic, morphological and grammatical forms, freed from their taxonomic function, are dislocated within a complex

---

[1] J.L.BORGES, *Tutte le Opere*, (ed. D.Porzio), vol.I, Milano 1985[4], vol.II, Milano 1985; the quote is from vol.II, p.57.

phenomenology which – opening vast horizons on mannerist behaviour in literature – redraws the very context of the problem of aesthetics. In such a phenomenology one can aptly give prominence to the "intellectual" reasons of *poiesis*, the almost scientific "coldness" of creating, and at the same time, asserting the necessity of conceiving an idea of poetry as free from any oneiric characteristics and randomness. Of course, this all can refer as well to a possible tropology concerning the very laws of the symbolic construction of the world. In such a context, the cold intellect does not *name* things, it utters them and evokes them. And this does not mean escaping into the irrational or the ineffable; on the contrary, it means defining a poietic engineering capable of constructing relationships that are not concretely named but only suggested. Mallarmé spoke of hidden correspondences linked and combined by means of logical-linguistic permutations. The calculation of such mechanisms and the methodic criterion which governs their variations, cannot but be turned against the randomness of inspiration and the psychological and sentimental suggestions of the world of life.

The poet is the *operator* who has at his disposal sophisticated combinatory techniques; he is the master of that "alquimia de la palabra" of which Lullo speaks; he is the *engineer* who is aware that through "processes of deviations groups of verbal sequences are obtained,"[2] so that – as Hocke has observed in relation to the *Ars combinatoria* in Mannerist literature[3] – a "group of words can be interpreted or permutated in a simple fashion. In this way for

---

[2]G.R.HOCKE, *Manierismus in der Literatur* cit. (p.59).

[3]Ibid.

every verse one obtains many adjacent and marginal linguistic areas, and, correspondingly, many meanings; in this way only single combinatory pieces are formed. They are joined in sheaves. The language continues combining.... even automatically." It is of little import here if "Lullism," in its manifold issues, has been transformed into a sort of universal method for comprehending the divine first cause of the world or if it has gradually been modified in the direction of a mysteriosophic or alchemical knowledge. Instead, what is important is to note how its "laws" have marked vast areas of Western poetry and have strongly influenced some of the most significant courses of aesthetic reflection in the modern age, from the Baroque to the twentieth century. These "laws" have meanings and relations that have redrawn *ab imis* ancient notions and categories. Suffice it to think of the concept of *figure* which is essential part not only in "formalized" and "organized" poetry but also in *poiesis* intended as active movement that convulses – to use Valéry's image – fixed vocabulary, operating through symmetries and exchanges of the very meaning of words.

In the *figure* poetry *presents itself* as an operation closely connected with the innermost being of language, in the sense that it does not *force* language but – as Genette has observed – corrects it, i.e., rewards and recompenses, fulfils or suppresses and ultimately *fills* it. Such that, "far from distancing itself from language, it constitutes and fulfils itself precisely *in its defect*, in the very defect that constitutes it."[4] In *Crise de vers*, analyzing the

---

[4]G.GENETTE, *Figures*, II, Paris, 1969, (It. trans. F.Madonia, Torino 1985 [2], p. 111-112).

radical imperfection of language attested by the "diversity of idioms" and by the distance which exists, in words, between resonance and meaning, Mallarmé[5] shows how there is no *speech* capable of totally expressing "objects with touches corresponding to them in colour and pattern." If there were, *verse would not exist.* Verse exists, in order to compensate – albeit illusorily – "the arbitrariness of the sign, that is, to *motivate language,*"[6] but above all to reveal the unknown hidden beneath the appearance of things, and to create ever new *harmony* between what it *says* and what it *is.* This *harmony,* which for Valéry consisted in a continuous combination of *sound* and *meaning,* lives in a game of inventions and requires the construction of an intellectual machine capable of posing and resolving a great number of problems, of stimulating the power of verbal invention that generally is quite unlike ordinary language and of realizing conventions. Thus certain "conditions" in poetry greatly reduce the indeterminate.

A fragment, a phrase or a verse behave as though they were endowed with a life of their own; through contrasts and symmetries, they "determine" the work, the character of which is that of a compact mechanism and, at the same time, an architecture capable of fusing heteroclite elements in a system of mysterious combinations, which realizes a *state* rather than a *particular form,* "a degree of presence and of intensity to which any enunciation.... can be raised, on the sole condition that around it a *margin of silence* be

---

[5]OC., p.363-364.

[6]G.GENETTE, *Figures,* II, cit. (p.113).

established that isolates it within daily language without however alienating it therefrom. This is probably why poetry distinguishes itself from all the sorts of styles, with which it shares only a certain number of means."[7] In fact, by taking us far from ordinary language, poetry tends to transform every thing, even *arid grammar*, into that "evocative magic" of which Baudelaire speaks. This process, however, does not require any degrammatization of language; on the contrary it finds in the modes and structures of grammar and syntax the web of a universe of "secrete identities" and enigmatic correspondences, which combine on the plane of a *lexical imagination* that orders the essential, the accidental or circumstantial and the relations within a *poetic syntax*, intended as the art of the *perspective of thought*.[8]

2.   Under the influence of Bentham, for whom linguistic fictions owe their existence to language alone and above all to the "grammatical form of speech," Jakobson[9] has offered us important research materials and theoretical indications that allow us to reexamine critically the "obligatory" character of grammatical processes and concepts, their indispensable, binding role (which, among other things faces us immediately with the intricate problem of the relationship between referential value, cognitive value and linguistic fiction), and, finally, the "poetic reason" of figures which fundamentally *say* that the

---

[7]Ibid., p.119.

[8]C.,I, p.414.

[9] R.JAKOBSON, *Poetica e poesia* (It. trans. R.Buzzo Margari, Torino 1985, p.341).

poet "does not affirm anything, and so never lies," because his *fictions* are "pure of insincerity."[10] The poet's fictions are modes of being, structures of grammar. Grammar, in turn, is analogous in import to composition, which plays an essential role in painting, "based on a latent or manifest geometric order or on a revolt against the geometrical arrangement."[11]

Grammar and composition, in short, represent a sort of "necessity" which regulates and governs both the art of the word and that of visual representation and figuration. The analysis of this *necessity* (and here the reference is particularly to so-called "grammatical texture") allows one to grasp important clues and subtle formal variations; and above all to trace the modalities through which a poetic work exploits "the available repertoire of the processes of technical mastery for a new end, and revaluates them in the light of their new tasks."[12] Used in this fashion, words, grammar and syntax never make merely indifferent referrals to reality, but acquire their own self-sufficient "truth," which defines the proper essence of *poiesis* as the territory of pure invention, infinite combinatory play and *fictio*. Poetry reveals itself therefore as falsehood. Fundamentally falsehood.

It matters little even if the artist claims that his work is inscribed under the sign of *Dichtung* or of *Wahrheit*: a poet "who does not start lying without

---

[10]Ibid.

[11]Ibid, (p.346).

[12]Ibid, (p.349).

any scruples from the first word is worth nothing."[13]   This concept of falsehood which – it is worth specifying – does not in any way refer to a possible logic of truth, thus figures as the typical problem of a specific area of literary civilization (consider, for example, the notion of *Lügendichtung*) but is also the fundamental structural characteristic marking the movements of *poiesis* in the multiplicity of their becoming. Ulysses is praised by the gods and men because he possesses the power of falsehood, bearing witness to the force of his shrewdness and talent; the gods themselves give mortals examples in this art. In the Homeric world, however, falsehood is not yet a problem. It will become so later when philosophers begin to be scandalized by it. First of all Plato, who accuses the poets of lying: their language – he says – is that of impropriety and untruth; and it is decisively different from the word of the philosophers, which speaks the truth.

Concerning this it has been observed that Plato's reproach of poetry means that in comparison with the "sincerity of philosophy, poetry is falsehood or at least truth obscured, and in any case a philosophical exegesis is necessary in order laboriously to harmonize the fiction of the poets with the pure doctrine of the masters of wisdom."[14] Hence, *poiesis* is brought back onto the plane of abstract *teorein*, of pure knowing. It is necessary, instead, to place oneself outside every paradigmatic gnoseologysm, and to think of

---

[13]Ibid, (p.44).

[14]H.WEINRICH, *Metafore e menzogna:la serenità dell'arte*, (It. trans. P.Barbon, ed. L.Ritter Santini, Bologna 1976, p.189).

falsehood as an aesthetically productive *fictio* or play of the mind. It is as one of the actual modalities of poetic making, determined essentially in the movements of the relations, signs and metaphors, alliterations and figures that it implies and in the forms it *says*, in which are realized – beyond the subject who sets their mechanism in motion – events and structures that acquire their own values and meanings. The Dadaists and Surrealists leave the writing of their verses to chance; Novalis finds the highest level of poetical composition in the letters of the alphabet; Mallarmé introduces us into the universe of modern lyric poetry through the senseless play of writing. All of these, even though in modalities that are not univocal, express an idea of poetry as artifice, combinatoriness and soulless "composition."

Such an idea leads us to reflect anew on certain salient features that characterize Baroque aesthetics. It is sufficient to consider the concept of *analogy*, closely allied to the artifice of conceit, which sets up a harmonious correlation among objects, things and events. Therefore analogy, which gives rise to an immense number of concepts, has no limits. As Gracián says, from analogy "emanate the similes and dissimiles of concepts, the metaphors and allegories, the metamorphoses and epithets,.... In these concepts, the subject is not linked to its own constellations but to some extraneous term, like an image that expresses its essence and represents its properties or effects, causes and occasions, and every other affinity..."[15] When the subject approaches this *extraneous term*, it almost disappears.

---

[15]B.GRACIAN, *Agudeza y Arte de Ingenio*, Huesca 1648 (It.trans. G.Poggi, Palermo 1986, p.63).

What remains is the memory of an initial movement which, perhaps, *continues* in the contrasts or mysteries, correspondences and symbols of this extreme experience, i.e. poetic making. This experience entrusts its destiny to words that have a seal analogous to those spoken by the Sibyl with the mouth of folly mentioned by Heraclitus[16]: they do not smile nor have any embellishment nor any perfume. They do not tell, they do not conceal, but they *signify*.[17] What? Themselves. Here the traces and the fragments of the world do not appear as moments of a "still unfinished discourse," but as that language by which – we could say with Blanchot – the enigma "is released from the intimacy of its secret to expose itself, in being written, as the very enigma which writing maintains."[18]

The enigma implies that writing (viz., poetic speaking) belongs to a language nobody speaks, addressing nobody and revealing nothing. Nevertheless, as Heraclitus says, it *semainei*: it hints, signifies or moves.

3.   The world of art – coherent construction, lucid fabrication of "new" realities realized within the patterns of conventions and combinations – bears witness to something that logical thought is not able to display: a "feast of the intellect." In the last pages of *Eupalinos*, Socrates recalls having sought God

---

[16]HERACLITUS, *I frammenti e le testimonianze*, (ed. C.Diano and G.Serra, Milano 1980; cf.Fr.119, p.53).

[17]Ibid., (Fr.120).

[18]M.BLANCHOT, *L'entretien infini*, Paris 1969 (It.trans. R.Ferrara, Torino 1977, p.229).

all his life, pursuing him only through thought. But the god he found is nothing but a word born from a word and returning to a word. Since – Socrates continues – each reply we formulate to our queries is nothing but the question itself, it is only in acts and in sets of acts, that we must find the most immediate sense of the presence of the divine and the employment of that part of our forces which may, perhaps, be useless in life, but seems reserved "à la poursuite d'un objet indéfinissable qui nous passe infiniment."[19] What is the universe – Socrates wonders – if not the effect of some act, and that act, in its turn, the effect of a Being, of a need, of a thought, of a science and a power that belong to that Being? It is only through an act that a great project can be accomplished or that one can resolve to imitate Him who has created all things. Now, the most complete act of all is *constructing*. And the construction of a work requires love, meditation and above all the capacity to invent laws and to draw from soul much more than one imagined or possessed. That is why each work, even though it gushes from the depth of the soul, is not to be confused with us.

In another part of *Eupalinos*, after having asked himself whether there exists anything more mysterious than clarity or more capricious than the distribution of lights and shadows in the hours and in men, Socrates states that for the Greeks – unlike what occurs among other peoples who lose themselves in their thoughts – all things are "forms." Of these only the relations are preserved, on the traces of which, through words, the Greeks have, in fact,

---

[19]O.,II, p.143.

built temples of wisdom and science. It is an arduous art, demanding a prodigiously exact language. Its name designates both *reason* and *calculation*, or rather, a calculating reason, one that seeks equilibriums, correspondences, and in doing, realizes forms. But realizing forms basically means reconstructing our person *ab imis*: "By dint of constructing," "I really believe I have constructed myself." In short, he has realized *another self*, which is located within objectivity where, moreover, all the realizations of the spirit are arrayed. The *other Self*, then, is none other than the work, the structures of which are analogous and contiguous with those that characterize the figures and the modes of the *poiein*.

The construction (or re-construction) of the I thus takes shape as a course which, passing through manifold strategies and manoeuvres, defines the contexts of the arts, the irreducible alterity of doing. The I, in fact, measuring itself with heteroclite materials (and language is a "material") and making use of them within a regimen of rigorous technical conventions, tends toward a pure form having value of its own and being altogether distinct from the multiplicity of the constitutive processes of *poiesis*. As regards the poetic word, it should be observed that, albeit dominated by particular conditions and a conscious musical feeling that is continuous and constant, it finds itself in a constellation of sense in opposition to that of ordinary language: here it is preserved, here it remains identical and unalterable even by very act of intelligence itself.

Thus the poetic word creates for *itself* a vocabulary, syntax, licences and inhibitions, to the point of "constituting a system of connotations as different from practical language as are the artificial languages of algebra and chemistry."[20] This "system" also clearly defines the difference between the person who observes and interprets the variations or symmetries, metaphors and all the *figures* of *poiesis*, coordinating them on a taxonomic and classificatory plane, and the other person who, instead, operates on the word, inventing and deviating. But in no way does it follow from this that any swerve and arbitrariness is permitted to him. On the contrary, it means that it is the task of the artist to find swerves and ruptures, which enrich, giving the illusion of power and of *pureté* or a *profondeur* which sinks its roots in the obscure gestures of the word.

Poetry, in short, is an artificial act, addressed, certainly, to making use of the dominant laws of language, but to "utilize" them against nature and history, so as to arrive at the "*repose*" of "*unreality*," which exists "only by virtue of the word," and the orders of which "lie in a wished-for, unresolved tension in relation to what is current and safe."[21] So, the over-abundant, excessive word, that renders the Baroque style particular, the artificial construction and the vocabulary without a subject are the most significant features of the whole course of modern poetry; they define its co-ordinates and deep reasons. In the seal of the soulless word we can, perhaps, grasp to what

---

[20]Cf. O.,II, p.1264.

[21]H.FRIEDRICH, *La struttura della lirica moderna*,(It.trans. P.Bernardini Marzolla, Milano 1983 [2], p.224).

degree "reality, dismembered or torn by the violence of the imagination"[22] lies in *poiesis* as a field of rubble, over which *forced unrealities* arise. But rubble and unrealities "bring mystery." The Baroque analogies and correspondences, Novalis' writing, Baudelaire's symbols, as well as the modern dissonances of poetic language are like the keys of a piano, which, however, only poets play. "Alone with language. But it is also only Language which saves them."[23]

From what? From the formless chaos of life, from the demands of the emotions, from the disorder of "rough reality." It saves them by leading them back not to the undefinable regions of the Unknown but to that realm of symbols and metaphors Baudelaire called *the dream*. The word "dream," however, should not here be associated with the naive oneirism of certain late seasons of Romanticism or certain poetics of *rêverie* of the twentieth century. It designates, rather, a construction by the mind, which, being perfect "like crystal" and free from the nets of categories, excludes any *real* inference. In the dream there are inorganic forms, artifice and dissonant tensions which, through the images of an empty ideality, achieve an extreme spiritualization. Baudelaire has drawn in exemplary fashion this cold landscape of poetic *inventio* in *Rêve parisien*.[24] Evident yet extremely subtle threads connect the

---

[22]Ibid, (p.225).

[23]Ibid, (p.225).

[24]Ibid., (pp.54-55).

design of this landscape with the most fertile intentions of Baroque aesthetics.[25]

Baudelaire's terrible, inhuman dream, is inhabited by frozen figures. No sun shines upon those prodigies. Everything shines with its own light and reveals its radical extraneousness from all the forms of the human. In this landscape of symbols, the I has almost been *wrought* and integrated into a system of defined relations and images. In the presence of the *other*, which it itself has produced, the I "changes," i.e. splits and multiplies or drowns. It has lost the power to direct and control its product which, freed from the linear, *logically* determined bonds of linguistic syntax, has arrayed itself on a meta-subjective plane, measured by simultaneities, immediacies, and free play. This does not mean poetry is in a "state of crisis." On the contrary, this "situation" testifies to the super-abundance of the I, which, in its infinite proceeding, almost achieves its own "emptying."

In the strategies it finds and invents and puts into play, the I tends continually to transcend its own boundaries. *Transcending*, can, however, mean providing "the proof of a transcendent presence in the edifice of the word,"[26] so that *Poiesis* as such ends by dissolving in the "terrible vicinity" of an incommensurable Logos. It is clear that this route leads towards a mystical, Neo-Platonic bourne, the basis of which lies in "certainty regarding a divine

---

[25]Cf. C.BAUDELAIRE, *Les Fleurs du Mal.* in *Oeuvres*, Paris 1973 (It.trans. L.De Nardis, Milano 1983, p.195-197).

[26]G.STEINER, *Language and Silence*, Cambridge 1958 (It.trans. R.Bianchi, Milano 1972, p.57).

meaning which exceeds and envelops us."[27]   But *Transcending*, in the theoretical perspective we are attempting to delineate here, means *constructing poiesis* as language – language which assumes the appearance of one of the modalities of the I, as the place, ultimately, where, from the splinters of subjectivity the "new" is born, which offers itself as metamorphotic form, measured by the cipher of its self-aim.   Such an idea of *poiesis*, on the one hand, seems to tell the tale of a subject that has foundered in the mad attempt to turn itself into *pure spirit*, devoting itself to the absurd and to folly (consider, in this regard, the figure of "Solitaire" one meets in *Mon Faust*[28]); on the other hand, however, it tells the ways by which the mind creates, producing forms and determining events, movements or situations, and, in so doing, continually opening itself to questions.

This idea of *poiesis* re-invents itself in the incessant play of language, which, in fact, is an instrument of discoveries or, better, an instrument for deducing and presenting "rigorous" observations and discoveries. That is why it becomes a *second nature of the mind*, in the sense that it multiplies the functions of consciousness itself and prepares and produces operations which "cohere" by virtue of a logic of their own, decidedly different from that sustains *pure thought*, thought without language, the *telos* of which is directed towards being and the absolute.   However, between "thinking" and "expressing thought" there lies only a nuance, in which contains "every possible philosophy" and every literature, and where, perhaps, lie hidden the

---

[27]Ibid.

[28]Cf. O.,II, p.385.

reasons that define poetic making as astonishing *inventio*, which, among other things, enables the mind to make its infinite exploration of the domain of knowledge beyond the word and – I would add – in spite of the word. By identifying the weft underlying that "nuance" one can proceed to attempt to grasp the "property" of *poiesis*, its logical syntax and its formal structures. i.e. its being event, whether movement or writing and its *being signified*, finally, as Form.

4.   But the *form* (or structure of sense) changes when one passes from poetic "composition" to its "translation" into prose. What is the reason for this "change" and how does it take place? And further: what is the *form of the sense*, which defines, more than eurhythmy and euphony do, the very being of *poiesis*? Starting from these questions, Jean Cohen, in his fundamental work, *Structure du langage poétique*[29] has reconstructed the problem of the "poetic," in the first place by identifying that "which form is not." Form is not substance; it cannot be determined on the basis of extralinguistic reality, or the thing, in its wide sense, to which language in any case refers. The thing, considered in itself, is not poetical. This does not imply that it is prose: it is neutral in its relationship to the prose-poetry pair. "The decision pertains to language." But language refers us back to things and, as far as poetry is concerned, outside of musicality "it does not possess anything not conferred on it by things." Consequently – Cohen notes – "things are poetical only

---

[29]J.COHEN, *Structure du language poétique*, Paris 1970, (It.Trans. M.Grandi, Bologna 1974).

potentially, and it is the task of language to actualize this potential"[30]: as soon, in fact, as reality is translated into words, it "entrusts its aesthetic destiny to the hands of language." [31] This means that in poetry a relation is established not with things expressed through language but with writing and verbal artifices, *inventio* and *figures*.

Etienne Souriau, in *La correspondance des arts*, had brought out the weakness of the arguments of those who maintain that only a universe composed of moonlight,   morning mists and forests, of symbols and mythologies of various sources, is *poetic*, whereas today's world, with its images, factories and metropolises is *unpoetic*. In agreement with Souriau's thesis, Jean Cohen stresses how not only the poetry but also the aesthetics and the poetics of our time have finally closed the accounts with so many *idola* proper to a certain humanistic tradition, introducing within the *horizon of the poetic* beings and things, which "it seemed were to remain excluded from poetry through a sort of natural curse."[32] These forms have instead proved themselves worthy of dwelling, with full rights, in *poiesis*, as soon as words granted them access to it.

This was a theoretical acquisition of great moment, which was made possible because aesthetics adopted certain points of view elaborated by linguistics. Just as linguistics, in fact, has explained language through its own

---

[30]Ibid, (p.63).

[31]Ibid, (p.63).

[32]Ibid, (p.64).

modalities, so aesthetics has read and interpreted *poiesis* in terms of certain specific forms of language. It has thus discovered that the poet is not a poet because of what he has thought and felt, but because he has spoken, since it is not with *ideas* that verses are made, but with words. The poet is not to consider himself a creator of ideas but a builder of words, an architect of verbal invention. Invention has at the most an extrinsic and inessential relationship with sensitivity or with depth of feelings. Feelings can do no more than provide some conventional indices capable of displaying manifold solicitations and stimulations. In short, invention occurs in those unique lexical combinations that make it possible for the sonorous verbal forms to achieve their poetic specificity.

In this regard, Cohen, examining a verse by Valéry "Ce toit tranquille où marchent des colombes," observes that if one does not understand that "toit" indicates the sea and the word "colombes" indicates some ships, then one misunderstands the poet's intention, which, nonetheless, has in itself nothing poetical (it is worth noting that Ricoeur agrees basically with this type of analysis[33]). The *substance* of the verse, in fact, can be expressed in another form and other words. The poetic fact starts from the moment when the sea is called "toit" and the ships "colombes."[34] In this violation of the code of language or in this linguistic gap lies the very essence of art, which, in the *figure*, frees "the poetic charge hidden in the world," kept prisoner by prose.

---

[33]Cf.P.RICOEUR, *La métaphore vive*, Paris 1975 (It.trans. G.Grampa, Milano 1981, p.198ff).

[34]J.COHEN, *Structure du language poétique* cit. (p. 68).

The figure, consequently, in violating the rules proper to the linguistic code, appoints itself essentially as anti-prose.

Hence, it is in prose that man's psychological reasons and emotions, i.e. his I, are preserved, whereas in the poetic figure – precisely because it is the pathological form of language – there is the negation or erasure of the I. Here ordinary language is brought back onto a plane where a sort of formal reconstruction is carried out, proceeding according to its own inner rules and, at the same time, with complete freedom, that is, outside the codices that characterize "ordinary" language. On this plane the *poetical objects*, i.e. the words, forms and gestures, are moulded in a "more perfect" way, so as to realize an inner coherence and density of meaning attesting to a continuous "adjustment" of the part to the whole and the whole to the part, *within* a combinatory movement that enunciates, asserts and *designates*.[35] In this movement the impressions and experiences of the artist are thwarted against the background of a distant memory. Eliot[36] was highly aware of this peculiar "condition" of *poiesis*, when he spoke of the creative mind as "a receptacle for seizing and storing up numberless feelings, phrases and images, which remain there until all the particles are present together that can unite to form a new compound."[37] Thus, the poet's mind can be compared to a filament of platinum, which produces sulfuric acid in the presence of two gases, without

---

[35]Cf., *Retorica della Poesia*, (It. trans. C. Donati, ed. A. Luzi, Milano 1985, p. 22ff).

[36]T.S.ELIOT, *The Sacred Wood* (It.trans., V.Di Giuro e A.Orbetello, Milano 1967, p.74ff).

[37]Ibid.

being itself minimally affected by the process it has produced, remaining "inert, neutral, and unchanged."

Poetic making, then, cannot but reveal itself even "without the direct use of any emotion whatever." Consider Canto XV of the *Inferno* (Brunetto Latini), where "effect" is "obtained by considerable complexity of detail." "The last four verses give an image, a feeling attaching to an image, which came by itself, which did not develop simply out of what precedes, but which was probably in suspension in the poet's mind until the proper combination arrived for it to add itself to."[38] Eliot's analysis, then, in spite of certain of its spiritual conclusions, demonstrates some indications that are extraordinarily kindred to those of prominent symbolist poetics (Mallarmé, Valéry) addressed to grasping and "fixing" the characteristics of *poiesis*, especially its *being signified* beyond the modalities of its being constituted.

The combinatory play becomes a movement which spreads states and emotions, produces sorceries and spells, but it does not communicate ideas. Such movement, freeing us from the confusion of values, the common and composite vision of things, and the monotonous disorder of external life, creates for us the illusion of proceeding towards the formation of an object having its own consistency, which presents itself not as the receptacle of the improbable forms of the creative personality, but as a land charted by a pattern of relationships and meanings, capable of bringing something into existence; of producing the unexpected, the unforeseen, which detaches itself from the agent and possesses "its own autonomous existence."

---

[38]Ibid.

5.   At the conclusion of his study on *Hölderlin*[39] Jakobson notes how language as such, "with its mighty complex of words and compelling syntactic rules," plays – at least in the last phases of Hölderlin's Journey – an essential rôle – not as *discussion*, but as *poetry*. So that talking and meeting with one another are rejected by the great Romantic "as the mere vestibule of language."[40] Let us pause a moment at this interpretation by Jakobson which evidently takes its place in a different perspective from Heidegger's reading of Hölderlin. Analyzing, decomposing and recomposing the last "Scardenellian" poem, *Die Aussicht*, Jakobson helps us to sound the intricate and difficult terrain of *poetic saying* which, in its "last stretch" having encountered the purity of the Logos, closes itself within the cold universe of the soulless word.

In this poem Hölderlin has achieved the absolute, through a sort of erasure of the world, in which all reference to the time of history has gradually faded away. The only possibility left to him is to reveal to men the *Ur-welt* of perfection and happiness, that lies beyond the birth and the destruction of the historical worlds.[41] The *Ur-welt* is marked by a geometric perfection in many ways analogous to that of Plato's noetic universe or to the completeness of Hegelian *logic*.[42] But it is not on the ground of these problems that Jakobson engages Hölderlin; it is rather on the plane of linguistic *Vernunft* that he has

---

[39]R.JAKOBSON, *Hölderlin. L'arte della parola*, (It.trans. O.Meo, Introd.by C.Angelino, Genova 1982).

[40]Ibid, (p.64).

[41]Cf. C.Angelino's Introduction to JAKOBSON, *Hölderlin* cit. p. XIV.

[42]Ibid.

grasped its aesthetic-logical originality. In the use of syntax, language and words, in the formal equilibrium which "the greatest schizophrenic" succeeded in achieving in *Die Aussicht*, Jakobson, in short, has "penned down" the *logos* that governs poetry with its laws and principles.

But *penning the logos down* and grasping its variations and significant modalities has required a long, complex, intellectual manoeuvre and a highly sensitive use of linguistic-hermeneutic techniques and strategies. On the one hand Novalis, on the other the Husserl of the *Logical Enquiries*. The former taught him to place the inseparability of the poetry-language relations at the centre of his reflections on *poiesis*; the latter turned him towards the quest for, and construction of, *a pure grammar*. Just this need for a pure grammar (which, in some way, is contiguous with the idea of a *universal grammar*, as envisaged in rationalism of seventeenth and eighteenth century) would seem to still be quite productive and fertile.

In truth, Husserl speaks of a *purely logical grammar*, correcting, in part, the term "pure grammar," which appears in the first edition of the *Inquires* (it had thus been thought and expressly indicated as the analogue of Kant's "pure science of nature.")[43] Nevertheless, apart from terminological *specifications*, the idea of *pure grammar* (not "universal" however, in the sense of a science embracing and containing all grammars) enables one to grasp not only what Husserl called the "ideal frame" of every language, but the articulations, structures and syntaxes of plurality, negation and modalities in which very

---

[43]E.HUSSERL, *Logische Untersuchungen*, Halle 1922 (It.trans. Vols.I and II, ed. G.Piana), Milano 1968. See especially Vol.II, p.117-128.

particular formations of meanings and constellations of sense are formed. Such an idea of a pure grammar tends towards rationality in the authentic sense and, at the same time, to the constitution of a pure system[44] in which the symbols, metaphors and figures are determined as real objects "ruled" by the *regulae* that constitute the forms of the actual legality of *poiein*.

These procedures, addressed to defining the general framework of the modalities of the imagination and of artistic creation, show, finally, in exemplary fashion how the practice of writing is reduced to that vast combinatory play mentioned above, which is situated within a pre-existent system constituted by language.[45] Here certain combinations are drawn within systems instituted once and for all; fantasy itself opens passages through the secret arrangements of the diverse sensibilities in our makeup, and *inventio* is *inventio* only when it determines itself and wishes to "be invented." That is why the true creator is not he who invents but he who discovers, or who "invents that which *wants to be invented*,"[46] such that it can legitimately be affirmed that the "real surprise, the *infinite surprise* which is the goal of art, is not born of an encounter with the unexpected";[47] on the contrary, it depends on an arrangement, i.e. on a capacity to field particular strategies appropriate

---

[44]On this theme, naturally within the orbit of a treatment different from what we are attempting to delineate here, see Husserl's analysis in *Formale und Transzendentale Logik*, Halle 1929 (It.trans. ed. G.D.Neri, Bari 1966, p.120-121).

[45]Cf. O., p. 614-15.

[46]G.GENETTE, *Figures*, I, cit. (p. 240).

[47]Ibid., p.240.

to attain improbable relations, new fictions and combinations that lead to the formation of self-consistent objects, clearly distinct from the author, in which sound and meaning, the real and the imaginary, logic, syntax, transformations or symmetries combine in a soulless paradigm of absent things.

In a passage from his *Book of Unquiet* Fernando Pessoa wrote: "These are my morals, or my metaphysics, or myself. A wanderer in everything, even in my very soul, I belong to nothing, I desire nothing, I am nothing: the abstract centre of impersonal sensations, a fallen mirror which feels and looks at the truth of the world..."[48] The abstract centre of impersonal sensations: this concept does not only tell us Pessoa's "aesthetic" discomfiture: it offers us a pathetic vision of *poiesis* as the site of the oblivion of the subject. And it also tells us that in the soulless word and in the writing of excess and metaphor are gathered the dispersed fragments of the variety of the world. It is perhaps in these that the enigma of poetic making lies hidden. Which, to use a beautiful image, has been called "enchantment."

---

[48]F.PESSOA, *Livro do desassosegu por Bernardo Soares*, (It.trans. M.J.De Lancastre and A.Tabucchi, Milano 1986, p.172).

III

MYTH, POIESIS AND IMAGE

1.   The strength of myth, which Hegel called the "Pedagogy of human kind," lies in the universal significance it confers on its *forms*, a significance accessible to the immediate consciousness of primitive man. This is why all authentic mythologies contain a *logotimia*,[1] or "reason for the myth," that is to say its "absolute" content, which, developed freely in ancient Greece, is nevertheless known to all the peoples of the world. Consequently *logotimia* must be considered the frame of a pattern of relations that have gradually been established between various human groups and deep historical stratifications; seen theoretically it reflects "the universal significance of history lost in the infinity of nature."[2]

If, then, Myth takes on meaning within a system of formal relations "not having any human or natural significance beyond the actual fact of their existence,"[3] mythology goes beyond its own limits and places itself beyond images still bound to concrete experience, whence contemplates a world of concepts freed from such slavery and are freely determined in the constitution of their relationships. Even though mythology *in any case* seizes upon and expresses a certain historical reality, transforming it in its web (so that its

---

[1] M.LIFSIC, *Anticnyi mir* (*Mito e poesia*, Introd. by V. Strada, It.trans. G.Pagani-Cesa, Torino 1978, p.53).

[2] Ibid.

[3] Ibid, p.55. (Cf. V.Strada's Introd. cit., p.IX).

"visions" translate the infinite multiformity of the world into symbolic terms), *mythopoiesis*, in addition to the ways in which it has been articulated, becomes one of the sites of the imaginary. This meta-individual and atopical site, dwelling place of the *total image*, requires the neutrality and the erasure of the existent and, as Blanchot says, requires everything to "re-enters into the undifferentiated ground where nothing is affirmed, and to tend towards the intimacy of what still exists in emptiness."[4]

It is certainly true that the material of *poiesis* is what is proper to myth, "the result of a highly intense and general charge and a very long process of uninterrupted enrichments and adaptations," "the synthesis formed during centuries of cosmic dramas lived as human dramas, and of human aspirations lived as cosmic dramas and expressed in figures."[5] But, beyond its *historical* and anthropological truth, *mythopòiesis* is something more. First of all, it is a revolt of the imaginary against the existent, and in that revolt, as Lifsic has noted, is delineated "the bridling of chaos and the transformation of the negative grandeurs into positive forces of life."[6] Thus myths, collectively, can be thought of as forming a system of images that grow in a spontaneous way, that is, a *logotimia*, in the sense that this system "rests on the real content of the life of peoples."[7]

---

[4] M.BLANCHOT, *L'espace littéraire*, cit. (with an introductory essay by J.PFEIFFER, *La passione dell'immaginario*, It.trans. G.Zanobetti, Torino 1975[2], p.222).

[5] Cf. A.SEPPILLI, *Poesia e magia*, Torino 1962, p.426.

[6] M.LIFSIC, *Anticny mir* cit., (p.152).

[7] Ibid.

The figures and situations characterizing myths, despite their immanent constitution, are very ancient forms of *poiein*: in short, they are modes of the universe of poetry, archaic-instinctive modes, independent both of individual experience and any sort of personal-subjective arbitrariness. It is possible to read in them the phases of a perennial process of emancipation from all functional and compound determination. It should be observed at this point, however, that the expression *universe of poetry* is also mythological. It is a *Fable*. It is, therefore, inaccessible. "Les mouvements de notre pensée autour de ce nom – noted Valéry – sont parfaitement irréguliers, entièrement indépendants. A peine au sortir de l'instant, à peine nous essayons d'agrandir et d'étendre notre présence hors de soi-même, nous épuisons dans notre liberté. Tout le désordre de nos connaissances et de nos puissance nous entoure. Ce qui est souvenir, ce qui est possible, ce qui est imaginable, ce qui est calculable, toutes les combinaisons de notre esprit, à tous les degrés de la probabilité, à tous les états de la précision nous assiègent. Comment acquérir le concept de ce qui s'oppose à rien, qui ne rejette rien, qui ne ressemble à rien? S'il ressemblait à quelque chose, il ne serait pas tout. S'il ne ressemble à rien.... Et si cette totalité a même puissance que notre esprit, n'a aucune prise sur elle."[8]

In this sense, the idea of *poetic universe* can only be grasped on the intuitive plane, since the notion we have of it transcends logic. Then, as regards its origin, we can again agree with Valéry when he affirms that "in the beginning was the Fable" – and there it will always remain. Since, thus, the

---

[8]O.,I, p.866.

Fable is the beginning, myth is a model of abstract history; its action takes place in a superior world, or one preceding the ordinary world. Furthermore, being outside any historical course of events, the characters of myth – Frye observes – can do what they like and the things that take place in myth are things that happen only in tales, remaining in an autonomous literary world.[9] As fiction, myth offers the artist a ready-made frame, "abundant in ancient reminiscences;" it offers a structure of conventions, a self-sufficient universe that takes us away from "life." *Stating the forms* of art *also* means scanning mythology, that global body of creations the meaning of which cannot but be associated with the concept of the intrusion of mystery into the sphere of real life, bringing a rupture of the recognised order, an "irruption of the inadmissible into the bosom of the unalterable daily legality."

Yet myths, as such, are absolutely static. One passes through them disorientated and amazed, as in a "forêt de symboles," as Baudelaire put it. *Mythopòiesis* succeeds in giving new senses to its *forms* if it frees itself from the static presence of myths, or if these are "dissolved" on a plane of operations or transformations situated within a complex system of forces and relations, "of which the creative spirit is nothing more than meeting place." In such a *system* the words and images becomes constituents and founders of poetic making as a *telos* towards pure poetry. Valéry, for whom "beautiful works are the daughters of their form *which is born before them*," observes that the idea of pure poetry is an extreme idea, where there is a perennial

---

[9]N.FRYE, *Favole d'identità'.Studi di mitologia poetica*. (It.trans. C.Monti, Torino 1973, p.37).

transformation of thoughts, one into another, and where the play of figures refers one back to an ontologically guaranteed reality. In the transformations that take place in myth it is perhaps possible, more than anywhere else, to meet with[10] an idea, at once modern and ancient, of the artistic, which offers us the key to an original and audacious exploration of the phenomenology of myth and its combinatory logic: an exploration which, aside from certain "falls" of myth in contemporary culture (but does talking about "falls" have any meaning?), leads us to read the dynamics of certain figures and forms, which require, apart from a different grammar, a hermeneutics suitable for interpreting the signs and meanings of symbols in the difficult situation of the imaginary today.

2. In *La poétique de la rêverie*, Bachelard states that the link between imagination, memory and poetry, by situating the phenomenon of a cosmic childhood "in the realm of values," can restore to us a natural oneirism "which has nothing preliminary about it." It is a matter – he writes – of infancies multiplied in a thousand dateless images. *Rêverie* "shifts whole blocks of thought without worrying too much about following the thread of an adventure, and in this way is very different from dreams, which always want to tell us a story.[11] " The story of such a childhood (which he calls "cosmic childhood") is not dated by the psyche. "The dates are added later; they come

---

[10]Cf. G.GENETTE, *Figures* cit., I, (p. 321ff).

[11]G.BACHELARD, *La poétique de la rêverie*, Paris 1978 (It.trans. G.Silvestri Stevan, Bari 1972, p.116).

from others, from elsewhere, from a time different from lived time. The dates come from the time when we do the telling."[12] "Pure memory" restores to us a mythical and far-off world in which one can rediscover a "being previous" to our being, a perspective of *precedence of being*, a *being without becoming*: it is not associated with a date, but with a mythical memory that does not need the specifications of a social memory in order to be psychologically reliable.

In the play that is set up between imagination, memory and *poiein*, one can identify the co-ordinates of a phenomenological approach to poetical making, intended as the place of the transparent eternity of the unreal. This is without doubt an "ingenuous phenomenology," capable of offering no more than the conditions whereby the works can be given a "pure listening"; however, it marks out a set of problems not always adequately examined in depth, and it indicates how the intentionality of the poetic imagination as *ouverture conscientielle* of all true poetry may be oriented. One could talk in this regard about *Transcendental Fantastic*, in order to stress the "quality" of an imaginative power that is no longer the result of a product of images, the dead residue of perception or of memory, but asserts itself as the creation and invention of a new *sense* against the dark background of archetypes, and finally as "fabulation poétique première," through which one can reach the heart of images. Rilke wrote that works of art can only come from a person who has faced danger, or has consumed an experience to its extreme limits. Such an experience allows to be determined the different modalities of the imaginary. They appear to be oriented by a concern with making time "pass,"

[12]Ibid., (p.116-117).

by means of spatial form, "from the domain of destiny, fatal because entirely objective, to that of ontological victory."[13]

It is in this sense that one can state that the imaginary, far from being the residue of a pragmatic deficiency, is the territory of an "ontological vocation."Far from being a passive epiphenomenon, nullification or even vain contemplation of a completed past, it manifests "as activity which transforms the world, creative imagination, but above all as the euphemistic transformation of the world, intellectus sanctus, the ordering of being..."[14]

Having thus defined the lines of a phenomenological anthropology of the imaginary, it is possible to re-signify the image-consciousness relationship on a different cognitive register: that is, the relationship between the faculties of soul and the structures of poetic making. In this mobile relationship, in a perennial *fieri* or becoming, the imaginary, having emancipated itself from the world of objects and of things, which is inscribed under the sign of the "res exstensa" (where the spirit and the being it reveals result in a nothingness of insignificant duration) re-defines the idea of space which, far from being an *a priori* form of material alterity, appears as the *a priori* form of spiritual creativity. For which reason it must be deemed that if it is the objectivity that mechanically marks out the mediating instants of what Durand calls "our thirst," and if it is time that stretches our imaginary appeasement in a

---

[13]G.DURAND, *Le strutture antropologiche dell'immaginario*, (It.trans. E.Catalano), Bari 1972.

[14]Ibid.

"laborious desperation," it is the imaginary that freely, in every instant, rebuilds the horizon and the perpetual hope of Being.

Hence it ensues that what makes the "I think" something more than an insignificant epiphenomenon or a disparate nullification is none other than the euphemising per se of the imaginary, "against which no alienating, deadly objectivity" can prevail. That is why only in the imaginary, which knows how to add "the assimilating interest of the useful" to dead objectivity, "the satisfaction of the pleasurable" to the useful, and "the luxury of the aesthetic emotion" to the pleasurable, can one find that "soul supplement" that contemporary thought seeks anarchically amid the ruins of determinism. "After having semantically denied negative destiny," in fact, the imaginary cannot but situate thought "in the total euphemism of serenity and of philosophical and religious revolt,"[15] filling "the semiological void of phenomena with ontological weight," and, by virtue of its transforming action on the world, binding and joining the things in the heart of consciousness.

3.   Living an event in an image does not mean disengaging oneself from the event and not being interested in it. Instead it means letting oneself be taken, "passing from the region of the real, where we keep our distance from things in order better to be able to deal with them,"[16] to another region "in which distance keeps us": there we deliver ourselves deeply to ourselves. Furthermore, living an event in an image does not mean having an image of

---

[15]Ibid, (p.435).

[16]M.BLANCHOT, *L'espace littéraire*, cit., p.229.

this event or conferring on it the quality of the imaginary. Even if it *really happens*, in the image the event deprives us of itself and of ourselves, returning us not to the *absent thing*, but to absence as presence. The image does not come after the object; it is not a *consequence* of things nor does it define a distancing that is quantifiable or empirically measurable.

The distancing articulated in the rhythms of the image is, according to Blanchot, in the heart of things. "The thing was there, we grasped it in the living movement of a comprehensive action and, having become image, it has instantly become the ungraspable, the inactive, the impossible, not the same thing distanced but the thing as distancing, presence in its absence, graspable because ungraspable, appearing inasmuch as it has disappeared... In the image, the object again touches something it has mastered in order to be an object, and against which it has built and defined itself. But now that its meaning, and hence its value, is suspended, now that the world leaves it idle and thrusts it aside, the truth within it regresses, the elementary claims it, in an impoverishment and an enrichment that consecrate it as image."[17]

Thus, the imaginary is an area that renders possible the transformation of things into images which, in its turn, are nothing other than allusions to what is without a figure; it is form "drawn on absence," thus "formless presence of this absence." This is why the imaginary universe does not refer to a transcendent surrealism, to an "other side" of the world; it is fundamentally on "this side," which however is nowhere. *Being nowhere* is the "property" of that atopical space which we call the imaginary. It is – as

---

[17]Ibid., (p.223).

has been written – absence without a counterpart in presence, "which does not yet announce itself if not as its own dissimulation."[18] That is why the image, which finds its ground and its condition in nothingness, sets itself as the extreme idea, which keeps us apart from things, saving us, at the same time, from the blind pressure of this setting aside.

One could agree with Sartre that setting up an image "means constituting an object on the margin of the totality of the real, that is, it means keeping the real at a distance and freeing oneself of it, i.e., denying it; or, if one prefers, denying that an object belongs to the real means denying the real inasmuch as one sets up the object."[19] It follows that consciousness, in order to form images, must escape from the world, keeping it as a sort of nullified background. In this perspective the imagination, as well as a *de facto* characteristic of consciousness, is seen as an essential, transcendental condition of consciousness itself, which sets itself on a plane other than that of the meanings and the relations which manifest on the level of culture and historical becoming. In other words, the place of the imaginary is that impersonal transsubjective, metaempirical place where things deliver themselves to the "sovereignty of the void," to nothingness.

4. Valéry wrote that every work is the product of things quite apart from the author: "the true artificer of a work, in reality, is nobody." This does not

---

[18]J.PFEIFFER, *La passione dell'immaginario*, cit., (Introd. to *Lo spazio letterario*, p.XV).

[19]J.P.SARTRE, *L'immaginaire.Psychologie phénoménologique de l'imagination*, Paris 1936 (It.trans. E.Bottasso, Torino 1964, p.282).

mean that the artist is altogether absent from his work, but that the work exists as such only if it frees itself of this presence, and the author becomes a *poet* only when and if he ceases being a man to become a *machine*, an instrument of operations and transformations. This requires defining the modalities of the existence and the conditions of the functionality of the artistic object, and above all unraveling the knots of the impersonal and trans-historical problems posed by poetical making on its specific order, within the general conditions of thought and the imaginary, independently of their content.[20] The fantastic, the imaginary, are thus correlated to an "ever re-arising arrangement" against which all the world's expectations "cannot prevail."

Therefore, in artistic making forms, words and figures *signify themselves* in a sort of *compound*, a combination "precipitated" from a mixture, a finished and significant "modality" that detaches itself from the disorder, the formless and the very existence of things and objects, to be inscribed in an *elsewhere*, where a variety of elements accumulate "capable of organizing themselves in succession, arranging themselves with a view toward a certain compositional unity..."[21]

This is an *elsewhere* marked by an inexhaustible phenomenology of images that are emancipated here, being subordinated to their own unreality, so that, on the basis of its form alone, poetic making promises what it is not, objectively announcing the claim that such non-existing "must be possible." The non-existent (and here we borrow a concept of Adorno's) is as scarcely

---

[20]J.GENETTE, *Figures* cit., I, (p. 241ff).

[21]Cf. O,I, p.1491.

existent "as it is scarcely universal concept";[22] it is present as the idea of art which – to continue with Adorno – must be considered strictly tied to the state of singularity of the work, and represents the not subsumable, "which in its turn defies the dominant principle of reality, that of commutability."[23] Nevertheless, by constantly challenging the principle of reality, art "tends its hand in a gesture towards reality, to shudder and withdraw on contact with it. Its letters are signs of this movement. Their constellation in the work of art is the codified scripture of the historical essence of reality, not the reproduction of reality."[24]

5. The imaginary lives in and of the poetic word, which, to quote Barthes, is an "abode" "settled as a source in the prosody of implied but absent functions." With the abolition of fixed relations, a "vertical connotation" remains pertinent to the poetic word (here "word" is intended as "language," "writing," the image as creator of another reality). The word is an act without an immediate past, "an isolated gesture, which proposes only the shadow of the reflections connected with it, wherever they may be from."[25] Each word, beneath which lies a sort of existential genealogy, brought back to a level "pregnant with all past and present specifications," becomes an unexpected

---

[22]T.W.ADORNO, *Ästhetische Theorie*, Frankfurt am Main 1970, (It.trans. E.De Angelis, Torino 1975, p.120).

[23]Ibid.

[24]R.BARTHES, *Le degré zéro de l'écriture*, (It.trans. G.Bartolucci, Torino 1982, p.35).

[25]Ibid.

object, from which all the virtualities of language take flight, opening the way to another, meta-physical, reality.

When "poetic language radically challenges Nature, solely by the effect of its own structure, without recourse to the content of discourse or to the support of an ideology, there is no more writing, there are only examples of style, through which man exposes himself completely and faces the objective world without passing through any figure of history or of sociability."[26] This is the path taken by certain poetic words of the twentieth century, whose scansion reveals empty gaps and silent pauses which, in many cases, not only become indispensable for the accomplishment of artistic creation, but tend towards a sort of estrangement from language. To some, such estrangement has appeared to be a part of a more general loss of confidence in the expressive authority and stability of our literary civilization.

George Steiner quotes a highly significant passage from Ionesco's *Journal*: "It is as if, through becoming involved in literature, I had used up all the possible symbols without really penetrating their meaning. They no longer have any vital significance for me. Words have killed images or are concealing them. A civilization of words is a civilization distraught. Words create confusion. Words are not the word (*les mots ne sont pas la parole*)... The fact is that words say nothing, if I may put it that way... There are no words for the deepest experience. The more I try to explain myself, the less I understand myself..."[27] The condition to which Ionesco is referring is that of

---

[26]Ibid, p.38.

[27]G.STEINER, *Language and silence* cit. (p.72).

our civilization, distraught by words. It has devalued the act of written communication to such an extent that "there is hardly a way any more of making oneself be listened to."

Only in the explosion of the poetic word is it possible to set up something new, a sur-reality, where nature dissolves in a succession of verticalities (the poetic words) that put men in contact not with other men, "but with the most inhuman images of nature,"[28] i.e., with the original gestures of the imaginary. This argument leads us back to a concept of writing as the place that is no longer at the service of the word or of an idealistically guaranteed thought. With its strength, not dedicated to anything other than itself, writing opens poetic reason up to different possibilities, new erratic routes, an anonymous, distracted, deferred or dispersed way "of relating," and a way that challenges categories and values and insinuates the idea of radical change. Writing, from this point of view – Blanchot is right on this – is the greatest violence, "inasmuch as it transgresses the Law, every law, its own law."

---

[28]R.BARTHES, *Le degré zéro de l'écriture*, cit., (p.37)

IV

POIESIS AND THE TIME OF ANGUISH

Where we see a chain of events, the angel of history sees one single catastrophe "which without respite accumulates ruins upon ruins"; but he would like to awaken the dead and recompose the broken fragments. "But a storm is blowing from paradise, which has blown open the angel's wings, and it is so strong the angel can no longer close them."[1] In this storm, which, according to Benjamin, pushes the angel of history "irresistibly into the future," one can identify certain traits that permit us to trace the paths taken by the artistic forms of our time, where the enormous treasury produced by the "creative sensibility" has been gathered.

If, on account of the extraordinary modifications and transformations brought about by technology, the multiplicity of the current instruments of communication, the "continuous inventions" that have modified the very concept of art, one cannot satisfactorily predict the directions of the aesthetic forms of posterity, it is nevertheless possible to identify the territory of certain of today's artistic events that have determined a cultural situation completely new and, until a few years ago, unforeseeable. One must place oneself outside the prejudged decisions of the traditional philosophies in order to sound out the

---

[1]W. BENJAMIN, *Schriften*, Frankfurt/Main 1955 (*Angelus Novus*, It. trans. R.Solmi, Torino 1962, p. 77).

living experience of art, which today as never before, seethes with problems and tensions.[2]

The *return to poiesis* requires theories to be reconnected with the real context in which art *is made*, in other words with that complicated, difficult relation that forms the texture of the web of works in their historical period. Therefore, aesthetic research must first undertake the analysis of the *conditions* of making, that is, of the reasons beneath the long, patient encounter of the artist with what he wants to say, conventions, *regulae* of taste, the phantasmatic play of the imaginary.

Therefore, the return to *poiesis* means insight into the open, mutable, unpredictable situation of contemporary art, the *loci* of which are no longer those of the past, if it is true that the new "bearers of aestheticity"[3] have definitively challenged the idea of the universality of knowing and, with it, the whole monotheistic system of the *Beautiful*. The angel of history, set "irresistibly towards the future," has begun to pursue a course that can no longer be idealized. Apart from splinters of a Messianic era, he offers us the code of the now of poiesis, in which there the loss of those absolute values is *represented* that art has lost, because it has wanted too much to seek them. Here we are, then, on earth, since the heaven we have dreamed about has revealed itself a lie.

---

[2]Cf. L. ANCESCHI, *Ultima lezione*, Bologna 1981, p.7.

[3]Cf. F. FANIZZA, *Variazioni dell'estetico*, Napoli 1982.

In this situation of disenchantment, 20th century poiesis has gradually gathered up the broken wings of the fallen angel,[4] it has once more sought its *origin* and, at the same time, has looked to the future. In its painful course, the sense of its *decadence* has become ever more evident. This can perhaps be read as the utopia of a poetical making, which seems to want to "prevent the catastrophe by evoking and exorcising its image."[5] In its return to things, art has begun to redraw its *status ab imis*, no longer finding itself guaranteed by universal laws. On the one hand, it has disqualified the world of its old appearances; on the other, it has become aware of the fact that, in order to invent something "new," "new names, evaluations and verisimilitudes"[6] are not enough.

The century now drawing to its close is the age – as has been written – of unlimited possibilities. The "constructions" of science are extraordinary and tumultuous; man's own productive forces continually outstrip themselves; the most advanced technologies have eliminated distance, radically modifying the old notion of time; "the misery of all the earth runs before the eyes of the

---

[4]Cf. J.JIMENEZ, *El angel caido. La imagen artistica del angel en el mundo contemporaneo*, Barcelona 1982. Through a metaphoric and analogic reading the author, identifying the sense of crisis underlying the fundamental aesthetic ideas of our time, scans some of the most significant courses of contemporary art, from Rimbaud to Kafka, from Rilke to Apollinaire, from Chagall to Max Ernst.

[5]T.W. ADORNO, *Ästhetische Theorie* cit., (p. 48).

[6]Cf. F.NIETZSCHE, *Die fröhliche Wissenschaft*, 1887 (It. trans. F. Masini and M. Montinari, ed. G. Colli and M. Montinari, Milano 1971, p. 79).

residents of the metropolies,"[7] who see the past surpassed by the present "from every point of view." Thus the fate of what were considered necessary ideologies appears highly uncertain, their values are revealed as tottering idols, and the fact that in some quarters these idols are obstinately defended tells us that the twilight has already begun.[8] We have already crossed the boundary into posterity, characterized by the transitory, the fleeting, the contingent, by one half of art, the other half of which is the eternal, the immutable.[9]

On more than one occasion Valéry declared the necessity of setting aside the idea of *beau travail*, the "definition du Beau" and every other type of metaphysical theorization of art, which he felt could only have a documentary or "philosophical" value. According to the author of *Teste* the word *Beautiful*, albeit illustrious and suggestive, had to be locked away in the drawers of the numismatists, along with other verbal coins no longer in circulation.[10] The image of the numismatists' drawers suggested by Valéry,

---

[7]M. HORKHEIMER, *Dämmerung*, Frankfurt/Main 1974 (It. trans. G. Backaus; Torino 1977, p. 8).

[8]Ibid., p. 5.

[9]The transitory, the fleeting and the contingent, are some of the forms Baudelaire uses to define the idea of the *modern*. However while these categories of Baudelaire's have a meaning which is, so to speak, structural and metahistorical ("There has been a modernity for every ancient painter"; "in order for every modernity to acquire its right to become antiquity, the mysterious beauty which human life unwittingly puts into it, must be drawn out of it." Cf. Ch. BAUDELAIRE, *Ecrits sur l'art*, in the It. trans. by G. Guglielmi and E. Raimondi, Torino 1981, pp. 287-290) are here used to identify the specificity and the radicality of art of the present era.

[10]Cf. O. I, p.1241.

demonstrates in exemplary fashion how certain categories and values pertaining to the "Artistic Tradition" are in decline by this time, how they have a consolatory function, and how their configuration is that of empty aesthetic surrogates.

Adorno speaks of a "prescribed consolation, destined to reassure men who feel atomized also in time,"[11] to stress how in the current age certain genuinely traditional elements, and alongside these even important masterpieces of the past, end by degenerating "as soon as consciousness starts venerating them as relics, transforming them into components of an ideology which feeds on the past so that in the present everything remains unchanged or changes only in order to intensify its constrictive, rigidified character."[12] It should be noted in this regard that, if from a subjective point of view it is revealed that Tradition is unusable, since it no longer possesses any substantial value, from an objective point of view it nevertheless constitutes a space in many ways still binding and fundamental. One need only think of the language of writing, which is not at all an agglomeration of token symbols. In writing "the values of each word and each nexus of words receive their expression objectively from their history."[13] Whence it ensues that the quest

---

[11]T.W. ADORNO, *Ohne Leitbild. Parva Aesthetica*, Frankfurt/Main 1977 (It. transl. E. Franchetti, Milano 1979, p.30).

[12]Ibid. (p. 60), Adorno writes: "Tradition should not be abstractly negated, but criticized without ingenuousness on the basis of the current situation; in this way, it is constitutive of the present. Nothing is to be accepted with eyes closed only because it once had some value but, nor is anything dismissed only because it is past: time alone is no criterion."

[13]Ibid. (p. 32).

for something "new" that is *absolutely devoid of tradition* and tends to erase "what past can be found in the relation with things which one claims are pure, not obfuscated by the dust of what has collapsed,"[14] ultimately leads to a sort of *inhuman oblivion*, which makes one forget the traces of suffering accumulated in the history of things, words, colours and sounds.[15]

Therefore, returning to things, in contemporary aesthetics, means not only redrawing the relation of art to modernity but relating in a non-conservative fashion to the works of the past, from which strata are freed, by virtue of their dynamism, which throw light on the present, in a *correspondence* that does not return one to empathy and immediate affinity but which requires distance.

Of course, it is not in the *substance* of the works that the living element of tradition dwells but in what has been left by the wayside and neglected, i.e., the derivative or the surpassed, in what has grown *old*, that is to say the strata that "in preceding phases had remained hidden, and emerge only when other, atrophied ones are peeled away."[16] The *living quick* of a work, then, is to be sought within the movements which have articulated its code and which acquire meaning precisely in their open relation with tradition, which, if it is

---

[14]Ibid. (p. 33).

[15]Adorno notes that traditon "today finds itself faced by a contradiction which is insoluble: none is current, nor to be resuscitated, but when every tradition is extinguished, the march towards inhumanity has begun" (ibid. p. 33).

[16]Ibid. (p. 35).

to be protected "against the Furies of oblivion" must likewise be "torn from its no less mythical authority."[17]

In this regard Adorno has noted that today "advanced aesthetic consciousness converges with the ingenuous, whose aconceptual vision did not claim the right to have any meaning and, precisely on account of this, sometimes acquired one. But one cannot rely even on this hope. Poetry salvages its content of truth only when, while maintaining close contact with tradition, it removes it from itself. Whoever does not wish to betray the happiness tradition still promises in some of its images, the buried possibility hidden beneath its ruins, has to turn his back on tradition, which abuses that possibility and that meaning, transforming them into lies. Tradition can reemerge only in what ruthlessly rejects it."[18]

Only the relation art establishes with tradition today can define the mobile space of the *aesthetic* in an age like ours, which appears convulsed by that "métaphysique surprise" of which Valéry talked when he attempted to grasp the directions of modern knowledge, disrupted by the variations of science, surprised time and again by the furious activity of physics, and disturbed and threatened in its most ancient and consolidated customs. Confronted by such transformations it is time to ask, with Valéry, what does the *I think* become, what does the *I am* become? And, finally, what does that

---

[17]Ibid. (p. 36).

[18]Ibid. (p. 39).

null and mysterious verb, the verb *To Be*, which has made such a grand career in the void, become, or re-become?[19]

These queries challenge some of the institutional knots of philosophical reflection, the idols of the absolute and the ancient monotheism of knowledge, taken to be the sole, normative, doctrinal apparatus. Returning to *poiesis* and, therefore, to things, means no longer recognizing only one norm but a multiplicity of norms, since – one could state with Nietzsche – one god is not the negation or blasphemy of another god. Thus, unlike monotheism, which legitimizes itself in the faith in one normative god beside which "there are only false and untruthful gods," *modernity*, marked as it is by an inexhaustible polytheism of forms, modes and "values," in its "reappropriating" the world is present to us as the age in which man, lacking *eternal* perspectives and horizons, finds "the strength to create for himself eyes that are new and personal, ever more new and personal."[20]

2.   "Just as it once revealed the immobile structure of the objective world in the object, today art has to reveal the mobile structure of existence in the project."[21]   This is how, in tracing in *Progetto e destino* the lines of a phenomenology of the survival of art in the world of tomorrow, Argan defines a project for which art must provide the methodological model.   In art's

---

[19]Cf. O. I, p. 1255.

[20]F. NIETZSCHE, *Die fröhliche Wissenschaft* cit. (p. 134).

[21]G.C. ARGAN, *Progetto e destino*, Milano 1977, p. 70.

projecting there is a sense, an interest and a passion for life, which it is impossible to find "in the unexceptionable logic of technological planning." According to Argan, it is in the project, where the traditional processes of aesthetic making are rapidly being transformed, that the profound ethics of modern art is realized, devoted to "reforming" society from pure technologism and thus saving it[22] through new and unmatched intentions, different from those of other ages of the history of culture, when the fundamental problem of art was to have a concrete, effective presence in social life.

Even though Argan has succeeded in identifying the utopian, projective space of certain current artistic experiences, he has not grasped the deep reasons behind the unfolding of the forms of our time, in which the movement of art, albeit contiguous with the modes of technological society, presents itself increasingly as an autonomous making, a practice with no extrinsic goal to realize, defining itself within its own structures according to the logic of its own modalities of significance. Art is, in brief, a "realm" situated at the utmost limits of language. It is not only the site of the escape into oneiric landscapes, artificial paradises or revolt against the reality of smoky factories and inhuman cities, but it is the uninhabited land, to which one can accede "through abandoning what is customary, natural and living."[23] Mallarmé speaks of the "divine transposition" of man, who proceeds from the *fact* to the *ideal*. But Mallarmé's thinking is not Platonic, for his "ideal" has no

---

[22]G.C. ARGAN, *Salvezza e caduta nell'arte moderna*, Milano 1977, vid. in particular pp. 11-71.

[23]J. FRIEDRICH, *La struttura della lirica moderna* cit., p. 131.

metaphysical consistency; it is *nothingness*, le *néant*, a term that expresses the *being of art* detached from space, time and things. This is an ontological concept marked by its idealistic origin. What worries Mallarmé is the inadequacy of every real datum. "Only an idealistic conception can feel this inadequacy. However, when the ideally adequate, to which the datum is commensurate, is placed so high that no definition can touch it, it remains pure indeterminacy and must necessarily be called Nothingness."[24]

In this ideal the fate of modernity is consummated; it is deprived of the ancient values and no longer guaranteed by Tradition; whence the will to root transcendence in Nothingness, where it is possible to consider the absolute the pure essence of Being, the annulment of the real. Such a process of derealization (in the *Vorschule der Ästhetik* Jean Paul spoke of "free space in Nothingness") cannot but bring about radical changes in the phenomenology of artistic making.

In the *Mémoires du poète*, Valéry observed that it would be interesting to write, at least once, a work which in each of its *noeuds* showed all the diversity which may present itself to the mind and from which the mind selects the single sequence to be given to the text. This would involve replacing the illusion of a single determination, imitative of reality, with "that of the *possible-at-each-instant*."[25] The idea of *possible* defines the *proper* domain of art as the space of Nothingness, which is a limit within which perennial

---

[24]Ibid.

[25]O. I, p. 1467.

games of transformation and changes take place.[26] Nothingness is not the site of the loss of meaning; it continuously refers to the thing it refutes. Its ontological code is analogous to that which characterizes the "Grand Abstraction" Kandinsky spoke of,[27] which requires giving up the representation of external reality, in favor of a progressive *distancing* from the human and from things, which nevertheless does not make a "contact" with transcendence but rather tends toward a complete absence of contact. There is an ontological dissonance between *poiein* and transcendence. The word indicates a failure of contact between the Absolute and man.

It has been observed that Mallarmé has caught some glimpse of the absolute, but it never becomes full light; it remains "as eternalization through the word which has attempted the impossible."[28] "Nothingness, with its own isolation, has a place where it can take refuge, viz. in the word."[29] Nothingness expresses the course of *poiesis* towards abstraction and purity. This abstraction *is represented*, at its highest levels, in that "phenomenology of the dance" that constitutes what is perhaps the most daring moment of the poetics of Mallarmé and Valéry. In the dance, according to the author of *Hérodiade*,

---

[26]V. Genette according to whom "perhaps the hour wished for by Valéry has come, of all that field of sensibility that is governed by language..." (G. GENETTE, *Figures*, I, cit., p. 242). Further, read Valéry's scattered observations on the idea of poetic in O. II, pp. 985-1056.

[27]Cf. V. KANDINSKY, *Über das Geistige in der Kunst*, München 1912 (It. trans. G.A. Colonna di Cesarò, Bari 1968).

[28]H. FRIEDRICH, *La struttura della lirica moderna* cit., p.139.

[29]Ibid.

thought does not perceive objective primordial forms but its own essence, in which phenomena are withdrawn from their phenomenal nature and from the objective ordering of space and time.

"Reality is felt as inadequacy, transcendence as Nothingness, the relation with the one and the other as an absolute dissonance. What remains? Talking, which contains its own evidence in itself."[30] For Valéry, the pure act of metamorphosis is accomplished in the dance, in a perennial passage from the heavy state to a "subtle" state, up to the ineffable, the ultimate idea that defines a place no longer exposed to the damp air of time, freed from all that is ephemeral between today and tomorrow. Here the "temporality" of the work dies and dries up, receiving the "silent gaze of eternity."[31]

3.   Works of art "get old" – writes Lukacs in the *Prolegomenon to a Marxist aesthetics* – "according to the justness or just proportionality with which the historical-social essence of the struggle between old and new is seen";[32] and he adds that "the decisive reason why one work keeps on being effective while another grows old, is that the former grasps the essential proportions and orientations of historical development while the latter does

---

[30]Ibid.

[31]Cf. F. NIETZSCHE, *Morgenröthe* (It. trans. F. Masini and M. Montinari, ed. G. Colli and M. Montinari, Milano 1971, p. 231).

[32]G. LUKACS, *Prolegomeni a un'estetica marxista* (It. trans. F. Codino and M. Montinari, Roma 1957, p. 210).

not."[33] Clearly Lukacs, in leading the phenomenology of the arts back onto the plane of "history" and the "progressive" truth of the Fact, cannot but define the *transitoriness* of art as the weak relationship of the work with history.

In its *duration*, however, art reproduces its own past, placing itself in the *continuum* of events. Artistic universality thus consists in the "generalization of reality" that can be relived by the person observing the work, which is a form of self-awareness of the development of mankind. Thus, in Lukacs' late work, the problematics of the relation between transitoriness/duration and historical time/metahistoricity, which in the Heidelberg years had been at the center of his reflections and had suggested questions and perspectives of exceptional actuality and interest, congeals within a rigid, gnoseological schematism, which does not permit him to grasp the variations and becoming of artistic forms nor the sense of the questions posed by the poetics of decadence, phenomenological aesthetics and the reflections of Mallarmé, Baudelaire, Rimbaud, and Valéry, which have determined a radically new cultural horizon, the understanding of which demands analyses and structures that the "philosophies of history" have not always been able to provide.

Lukacs' rejection of the modern avantgarde and phenomenology of decadence is typical of a culture which, rising in the wake of idealism, has been unable to set itself outside the tradition, which, for centuries, has exerted a strong humanist and "literary" influence on knowledge. The observatory of

---

[33]Ibid., p. 211.

that culture has been history. But to consider art after Nietzsche and Husserl requires first of all that *poiesis* be faced from a different observatory. The historical philosophies make us "return" to the work, but the work is not an inert unity at rest but a web of intimate and violent movements that are never reconciled or at peace. Blanchot talks of *lacerated unity*, presence of being and of "event." "This event does not take place outside time; nor is the work only spiritual, for through it another time enters time, and into the world of beings who exist and of things that subsist enters, as presence, not another world but the other of every world, which is always other than the world."[34]

In the work, intending and speaking are composed into a reality in which the *poietès* completely dedicates his being. In this sense the poet does not survive the creation of his work, "He lives by dying in it." Thus the work, by the *logic* that sustains it, takes form as a sort of *monad*, with its structures, statute and internal "lawfulness." Withdrawn from the "dominion" of its creator it offers itself to its enjoyer who, interpreting it, tells it anew, but not as something repeated, already said and understood. Author and reader are peers in front of the work and inside it, since it is the creator who has been dismissed; "his name is erased and his memory extinguished. This means... that the creator no longer has any power over his work, he has been relieved of it, just as in it he is deprived of himself; he does not keep its meaning, its

---

[34]M. BLANCHOT, *L'espace littéraire* cit., p. 198.

privileged secret; he is not entrusted with the charge of 'reading' it, that is, of repeating it, of stating it each time as if anew."[35]

The work is nothing other than an event, which *poses* the problem of art; in other words, for the work art is never given, and the work "can only find it in its own accomplishment and radical uncertainty of knowing at the start whether art is, and what it is."[36] This means that the work is a work, starting from arts, it "states the beginning when it states the art that is at its origin, and the essence of which has become its task."[37] Its time *exists* before the world, *before the beginning*. That is why the work casts us "out" of our power of starting and finishing, turning us over "to the outside without innerness, without abode and without rest," in the "infinite migration of error." The time of art is the time of non-history; its kingdom is a godless place.

Blanchot talks of the *time of anguish*, image that designates the time that "emerges" in the work, when "the gods fail" and the world of truth vacillates. It is time placed on this side of time, the time of the poet, in short, the empty time in which the poet is obliged to experience "the twofold infidelity, of men and gods, and also the twofold absence of the gods, who are no more *and* are not yet. The space of the poem is entirely represented by this 'and' that indicates the double absence, the separation at its most tragic

---

[35]Ibid.

[36]Ibid.

[37]Ibid., p.213.

moment. But the problem of knowing whether it is also the 'and' that joins and links, the pure word in which the emptiness of the past and the emptiness of the future become real presences, the 'now' of the rising day, all of this is private in the work; it is what is revealed in the work by returning to dissimulation and the anguish of oblivion. That is why the poem is the poverty of solitude. This solitude is intelligence of the future but impotent intelligence, the prophetic isolation which, this side of time, always announces the beginning."[38]. The work states art on this side of time, and to state art means to produce singular, enigmatic events; it means to sing and to exist. Rilke writes, *Gesang ist Dasein*. In its perennial beginning the work affirms the *existence of things* that live in the *empty time* of the imaginary. The work contains levels and modes of reality other than those that "determine" the phenomenology of the concrete, registered in the path of *history* and full *temporality*.

4.   The institutions of art, in which various motives of intentionality *towards* poetry are articulated, mainly concern the art of making. Born out of the reflections of artists, the institutions of art propose ideals, principles and working concepts, and acquire their meaning "in the fact that, in general, however they are oriented, they tend to make use of all the aspects of reality it is possible to use, so that they are drawn up to make art ever more aware of itself, its making and the principles of this making, in the situation where,

---

[38]Ibid., p. 216. Regarding this one might read V. Vitiello on the concept of singular word in V. VITIELLO, *L'utopia del nichilismo*, Napoli 1983, p. 160.

over and again, it finds itself deciding for itself, establishing its own constituent choices."[39]

Thus, if on the one hand the institutions are measured in a *weak time*, associated with the time of space (this is the time in which we situate our acts, perform our practical needs and consolidate our habits), on the other hand they are ordered towards a pure *duration* that appears free of "tout mélange." The weak time is inherent in the technical structures and materials of the *poiein* and in its structural characteristics. Instead, in *pure duration* the modes of *poiesis* are represented and *signified*; it uses and rules its "material" by transforming it into events that gather all the manifold virtualities of *making*.

Taking their measure from the fast or slow rhythms of history, the institutions of art tend almost to become immobile in a timeless duration that lends itself to the most diverse analyses and makes an extraordinary variety of hermeneutical courses possible. Thus, the *poiein*, although "structured" in extension, succession and *things*, and it is fundamentally a "quality" that permeates human experience (it is nevertheless *also* a chronicle and a celebration of the life of a civilization), acquires its *sense* beyond temporality, on the "over here" which defines the realm Shelley spoke of, where subjectivity is the absolute and which exists only in a thought, an action or a person that is not *ours*.

Whence it ensues that poetics, even though it constitutes systems "for the ends of art," inasmuch as it chooses the most suitable among real

---

[39]L. ANCESCHI, *Le istituzioni della poesia*, Milano 1968, p. 21.

possibilities "in order that art relate to the complex situation in which it lives," and even if it continuously reveals its innate structures and intentions and the violence of the tensions running through it, always adds something to the world of which it forms a part helping us to enter "the obscure and forbidden labyrinthine passage where art is formed and born." In that passage a web of suggestive relations is determined "that does not allow univocal solutions, and which, on the contrary, helps to understand the life of art in the fullness of its meanings, in all the implications with all the other aspects of experience, for a totality of comprehension."[40] This web of relations is in a space open to all the manipulations of fantasy, where the *Gestaltungen*, the artificial configurations introduced by man and by "history" are dissolved, to use a Rilkian image, in the infinity of the open, which is a movement rich in expectation and continuously suggests ambiguous messages, improbable, multiple meanings and tensions towards universality.

In his *Discourse on Lyric and Society*, while identifying the "knot" that characterizes modern lyrical creation (this analysis can be applied to the whole phenomenology of poiesis as well), Adorno notes that the context of a poem is not simply the expression of individual experiences or motions. Individual experiences become *artistic* only if they participate in *universality*. This is not the universality of the pure communication of what others "are incapable of communicating," nor is it to be understood as a general *volonté de tous*. Upon *lowering itself into what is individualized*, lyric poetry rises "to universality,

---

[40]Ibid., p. 40.

because it manifests what is not deformed, not understood, not yet whispered, and in that way it spiritually anticipates something of a condition in which no evil, that is, deeply particular, universal any longer be allowed to chain the other universal, the human. Lyrical creation aspires to achieve the universal through unreserved individuation...."[41]

In this way Adorno offers us the key to the "particular universality" of poetics that are not self-born nor set up within abstract logical operations, but *are formed*, gradually, within their movements. These movements do not only reveal and *signify*, by means of laws, norms and instructions, the reasons for the artistic renewals of the various ages, but constantly set themselves as a challenge, exploration, *invention* and ultimately as radical risk. These poetics thus tend to be oriented towards a no longer present objectivity that has no solid abode but is situated at the limit of history.

Introducing the concept of *poésie générale de l'action des êtres vivants*,[42] Valéry grasps the site of the *idea of limit* in the dance. The dance isolates and develops the essential characteristics of the human body, whose transformations and infinite possibilities of movement express the *puissances instantanées de l'être*. The very *destiny* of art, at its highest levels, is to be found in dance. Dance embodies the work and metamorphoses that the poet

---

[41]T.W. ADORNO, *Noten zur Litteratur*, Frankfurt/Main 1958 (It. transl. A. Frioli, Torino 1979, I, p. 47).

[42]Cf. O I, pp. 1391-1403.

realizes and, at the same time, his distancing himself from the earth, the *moyens* and the logic of common sense.

The institutions of poetry, technique, language and "history" are the "conditions" which make *ars* possible, but they also constitute the reasons which take *poiesis* out of the "monde pratique" into the "lieu privilégié de la danse spirituelle." By virtue of their necessary presence, finally, the institutions, manifesting an unlimited expansion of artistic consciousness, disclose to us multiple universes that are not dispersed in chaos or in insignificance but appear "oriented" in the directions of the coherent organism of making. *Making takes us back to things*, it enables us to be aware, through things, of certain "graces" that have not yet entered the world.

5.   In the *Lettre du voyant*, with regard to the dualism, unresolved by the Romantics, between "thought sung" and "thought understood" by the singer,[43] Rimbaud writes "Je est un autre," so that if a brass wakes up as a trumpet *il n'y a rien de sa faute*... "I attend to the blossoming of my thought" adds Rimbaud, "I watch it, I listen to it, I tap with my bow, the symphony rumbles in the depths or leaps onto the scene with a jump."

An *other*, then, derived from the I, shatters the I's unity into a multiplicity of events, in whose movements things are freed from the "yoke of habit and of reason." But if I is an Other – Richard has noted – "it is nevertheless I who has produced this other, yet has *not* been able to produce

---

[43]V. Margoni's observations on the *Lettre du voyant*, particularly note 6, p. 403, in Rimbaud, *Opere* (trans. and introd. by I. Margoni, Milano 1980).

it, because this other is exactly an *other*, a radically new being, incomprehensibly alien; this thought is still, and more than ever, mine."[44] This is the paradox of the new *cogito*, which gives us the key to enter the Rimbaudian adventure. The mystery this poet addresses is precisely that of the passage or advent from the *self* to the *other*, by virtue of which "night is derived also from day, the past from the future and nothingness from being. It is the mystery of creation."[45] Through the paradox of this "*new cogito*," the very being of thought is challenged. It is false to say "I think," one ought to say "I am thought." The true subject is thus not the empirical I, since other, pre-personal powers take its place, posing themselves as the organs for the comprehension of the *Unknown*. Such a "collapse" of the I is manifest in the work of the poet, who is toiling "in the exploration of the world through a violent imagination."

Through his questions Rimbaud leads us to the thresholds of modern poetry, in which "new experiences, which the worn out material of the world no longer grants, surface" from the chaos of the unconscious.[46] Beyond these thresholds lies the ineffable silence of Absence, the cosmic totality. Rimbaud rejects the temptation of totality to rediscover his identity "in *a* soul and in *a* body." In his "return to things" he seizes again upon the solidity of reassuring

---

[44]J.P. RICHARD, *La creazione della forma* (ed. C. Bo, It. trans. G. Bogliolo). The passage quoted here refers to the essay *Rimbaud o la poesia del divenire*, taken from the vol. *Poésie et profondeur*, Paris 1955.

[45]Ibid., p. 347.

[46]H. FRIEDRICH, *La struttura della lirica moderna* cit., p. 64.

powers such as *strength* and *beauty*, which he rediscovers in the *weak time* of history. The *Je* returns to itself in the awareness that the *Autre* can never be reached. The subject, finally, "reconstructs itself."

But can one reach the absolute? Mallarmé had written "La destruction fut ma Béatrice." Destruction of the subject, then. Mallarmé speaks of a "longue agonie" in the course of which the individual I attempts to place itself outside temporality to arrive at the "région de l'Esprit" and to win its own identity as the center of universal reflection. Thought, thinking itself, arrives at a pure conception, which does not "happen" through abstract speculative analysis but involves the whole universe of the sensibility. The *Destruction* of the I is thus inscribed in a *fantastic dialectic* by virtue of which the I identifies itself with absolute thought, eliminating its individual determinations.

Such a dialectic, built through a "voie pécheresse et hâtive, satanique et *facile*" cannot but lead to the *oubli* of the I in a movement of erasure and awakening, or better, "d'éveil par l'effacement."[47] This is the "awakening" that surprised us when we discovered we were about to leave our "old world." But – one asks – what will *the world* be when we have definitively left it? Rimbaud would say, "en tout cas, rien des apparences actuelles."

---

[47]R. DRAGONETTI, *Aux frontières du langage poétique*, in "Romanica Gandensia," IX, p. 123, Gand 1961.

V

THE DIFFICULT RETURN TO THINGS

1.   The *state of poetry* is so irregular, inconstant and involuntary that is liable to become weakened, or even lost, by mere accident. It depends on a special psychological situation of the poet. Inasmuch as it is the poet's "private affair," *poetic state* must be distinguished from the artificial synthesis actualized in the work. *Une action suivie* is something far more complex than instantaneous production, above all "when such an action must operate in a territory as conventional as that of language."[1] Different from the *poetic state* and, at the same time, not referable to the forms proper to abstract thought (which, as such, is not a "producer" of verse), poetry is a *discourse* which, in a continuous process of transformation and modification of ideas, speaks of things absent or "deeply and secretly felt." A strange discourse which to Valéry seemed to be held by a character other than the person who utters it, and addressed to a person other than the one who listens to it. It ensues that understanding and interpreting a work of art means, above all, replacing a system of resonances and signs with *something else*, which cannot but affect a "modification or a reorganization within the person addressed."[2]

Being a language within a language, *poiesis* produces profound transformations, making us think according to different laws from those

---

[1] O. I, p. 1322. Vid. also C. II, pp. 1059ff.

[2] O. I, p. 1325.

marking "l'ordre pratique" and on the basis of a different theoretical statute; it *invents* situations that cannot be *fixed* in any determinate act. The means used by the poet were not created solely for his speech; the poet, according to Valéry, has to turn to the public word consisting in a collection of traditional rules created in the strangest ways, and of codified terms, understood and uttered in many ways. In other words, he must make his way among the phonetic and semantic oscillations of the vocabulary, where everything is impure and incoherent. Amid such vast lexical material, the poet is not only constrained by the musical period and harmony but also by the "conditions intellectuelles et esthétiques variées"[3] as well as rules of convention.

He thus *discovers* certain relations between things, where artistic creation "takes shape," the value of which, writes Genette, is measured by a criterion that "lies not in its novelty but, on the contrary, in its profound antiquity."[4] The artist must compose wisely compositions, obeying to the signs of conventional structures, which require the use of techniques and modes of expression giving the impression of a "series of magical transformations of the same emotional substance." In order to effect such transformations the poet, without losing any shading of fantasy, must submit to strict, almost inhuman rules, abstract laws and severe patterns.

In this a perspective, the freedom of art (not to be confused with certain of its superficial manifestations) is fulfilled only when it works its way through

---

[3] O. I, p. 1328.

[4] G. GENETTE, *Figures*, I,cit. (p. 240).

a network of terribly harsh conditions. These make possible the *invention* of what we call "works of art," which are always the result of an action whose *finite aim* triggers and generates manifold developments. The artist, recomposing the laws and means of the world of action, "en vue d'un effet à produire l'univers de la résonance sensible,"[5] must be considered "un être double" in the sense that only through the possibilities and limits of the *craft* can he activate the infinite processes of *poietic* transformations. Artistic work aims at the *production of things*, and requires the artist to have self-mastery and technique, as well as the capacity to ask himself the *right questions*, in the course of his work. In other words, the artist must know how to carry out "simultaneously an act which aims at precision" and another act capable of producing contemplation. The former refers to a *present* model, the second "refers to a hidden truth." The *practice of art* consists in maintaining a delicate equilibrium between these two acts.

In analyzing the "particular qualities" of the poet – être-*double* – and identifying the paths of the *practice of art*, Valéry has identified the forms and modes of a poetics which, on the one hand, intends to define what is *proper* to the work (its structure and levels of sensibility) and, on the other hand, sets the unsurpassable *limit* constituted by poetry. The poems and works, written or yet to be written, strive towards that limit, with respect to which they are merely fragments, rehearsals or preparatory studies.

---

[5]O. II, p. 1344.

2.   Valéry follows the thought of Mallarmé, who had sought to realize a *pure work*, which necessarily implied "the *elocutory* disappearance of the poet" who, in his turn, could not surrender the initiative to the words, "mobilized by the impact of their inequality."[6] In so doing, Valéry, as we have seen, considers poetic making to be a phenomenology of figures of transformation. In him, as in Mallarmé, the figures that mostly perform an accessory role in language, as it they were mere ornaments the substance of discourse could well do without, become essential elements. Metaphors, transformations and invention become fundamental relations.

In *Crise de vers* Mallarmé writes: "Parler n'a trait à la réalité des choses que commercialement: en littérature, cela se contente d'y faire une allusion ou de distraire leur qualité qu'incorporera quelque idée. A cette condition s'élance la chant, qu'une joie allégée."[7] According to the author of *Un coup de Dés*, the pure word will not be satisfied with a musical syntax; it must become a pure, abstract arabesque that evokes vague atmospheres of unfelt sensations and unseen images. It has been written the pure word has "the mysterious power to create around itself pure atmospheres and rhythms, in which vague sensations accompany unexplainable, gratuitous gestures, so that the demon of analogy designates the mysterious relations which the word, once having freed itself from any close connection to the practical, logical syntax of the phrase and to dictionary meanings, can relate to particular states of mood, by

---

[6]Cf. OC., p. 366.

[7]OC., p. 366.

determining gestures, musical rhythms and sensations absolutely separate from all concrete experience."[8] The Mallarmean *pure word*, creating analogies of things through analogies of sounds, is not all of being, but it is a sign of being: "Le Langage est le développement du Verbe, son idée, dans l'Être, le Temps devenu son mode."[9] It is not the *Original Utterance*, where both poetry-making and speaking belong, but it is the *extreme limit* to which *poiein* tends, constantly influenced by intuitions, correspondences and mystery. This *limit* constitutes the very meaning of *poiesis*, its truth.

In a letter dated 1907, Rilke wrote: "Thus, the objects of art are always a result of having-been-in-danger, of having gone to the end of an experience, further than which nobody could go. The further forward one goes, the more an experience becomes particular, personal, unique, and the art object is finally the necessary, irreprehensible pronouncement of such uniqueness, as definitive as is possible... The art object is of immense help to the life of the person who has to achieve it... it is his recapitulation, the rosary bead with which his life says a prayer, the ever-recurring proof, given for him, of his unity and truthfulness, which turns only towards him, while acting anonymously towards the outside as necessity, reality and existence... We are thus certainly obliged to contend with and challenge the Extreme, but also probably bound not to pronounce this Extreme before it passes into the work of art, not to share nor to communicate it. As an *unicum* nobody else would or could understand, as

---

[8]L. ANCESCHI, *Autonomia ed eteronomia dell'arte*, Firenze 1959 [2], pp. 241-242.

[9]OC., p. 854.

a personal frenzy, so to say, it must enter the work in order to acquire validity within it and indicate its law, as an innate design that becomes visible only in the transparence of the artistic fact."[10]

Apart from grasping the extreme form of the *poiein* in the idea of limit, Rilke defines the area of meaning of much modern poetry, which *gives itself* as thing, and *is signified* precisely in its giving itself as thing. The passage quoted refers to the work of Cézanne. The attention Rilke pays to the visual arts (especially, one should remember his *Rodin*) demonstrates in an exemplary fashion how his poetics of *Dinggedicht* arises from the question of the meaning and fate of things. In fact, the transfiguring violence the artist exerts on the data of experience is revealed in things; it is here that the seal of *poiesis* is rediscovered. But, it is well to stress that in the aesthetics of the *Dinggedicht* poiesis does not directly express the psychic and imaginary contents of the artist; rather it provides an external equivalent that allows one "to get back intuitively to the same order of inner realities (images, sensations, creations, etc.)"[11] that moved the poet.

3.   In Mallarmé as in Valéry poetry does not directly express the artist's reality. According to the author of *Igitur*, although the poet has at his disposal the same words as the person daily using the language, he erases life from the words in the construction of his semantic system in order to use them in "all

---

[10]R.M. RILKE, *Lettere su Cézanne*, (It. trans. G. Zampa), Milano 1984, p. 28.

[11]Cf. A. DESTRO, *Invito alla lettura di Rilke*, Milano 1979, p. 62ff.

the range of their possible correspondences."[12] In accord with Poe's motives and reflections, Mallarmé finds a space in the poetic word, where significant silences can be communicated, in which no philosophical, ethical or metaphysical "references" must be glimpsed. The word, from which all "intellectual armour"[13] must be erased or dissembled, is made of matter and light; nevertheless, it is incorporeal, it does not represent anything, it is absolute virtuality. The word, finally, which in the verse becomes total, "a stranger to language," incantatory, breathes a "neuve atmosphère"[14] over the things it utters.

Mallarmé speaks of a superior attraction "comme d'un vide" which detaches things, conferring splendor on them "à travers l'espace vacant, en des fêtes à volonté et solitaires."[15] The *espace vacant*, open to the poetic word, is the space of the poem in which the poet, things and language become vain and lose their "*existence solide et prépondérante*"; thus it is the very abode of poetry, which, albeit still rooted in the soil and dust where everything ends, strives toward the ideal. As Mallarmé writes about Théodore de Banville, "Ce cri de pierre" unites skyward through pillars broken by arches that have a bold

---

[12]Piselli, in his exegetic note on the *Opere in Prosa* of S. Mallarmé (It. trans. and edit. F. Piselli), Milano 1963.

[13]OC., p. 872.

[14]OC., p. 858.

[15]OC., p. 647.

prayerful *élan*, "mais enfin, quelque immobilité."[16] In poetry the word is not spoken but speaks being. Better put, it utters the impossibility of uttering being. Thus poetic language must be considered the only possible, fictitious place "de l'avènement de l'Être".

This means that human life is without a "safe" abode and is continuously checked by the doubt of the "Je suprême". Whence it follows that existence can only be an "interregnum" between a "passé en désuétude" and a "futur en effervescence". It is the interregnum of the absence of the god that demands the "proof" or "fiction," that is, literature, which is an ordered system with its own specific abstract doctrine "ésotérique comme quelque théologie," in which certain "notions" have attained a degree of rarefaction so far beyond the ordinary that they can only be expressed through typical yet supreme means, whose number "n'est, pas plus que la leur, à elles, illimité."[17]

Having thus defined the methodological-hermeneutical grid of his poetics, Mallarmé applies it to certain theoretical pronouncements "taken" from Descartes' thought, from whom, basically, he borrows the movement and the overall strategy. Which is Mallarmé's Descartes? It is the philosopher, for whom "all method is fiction": "Le langage lui est apparu l'instrument de la fiction: il suivra la méthode du langage (la déterminer). Le langage se réfléchissant. Enfin la fiction lui semble être le procédé même de l'esprit

---

[16]OC., p. 521.

[17]OC., p. 850.

humain – c'est elle qui met en jeu toute méthode, et l'homme est réduit à la volonté."[18]

Mallarmé's Descartes is the symbol of abstract reason, i.e., the pure word that survives the shipwreck which, in *Un coup de Dés*, drowned everything in the "identical neutrality of the whirlpool." The pure word makes the invention of ever new symmetries, transfigurations, inventions and correspondences possible. If the word tells of lack, deprivation and absence, it also refers to something else.[19] It not only opposes ordinary language but even the language of thought. "In this word we are no longer referred back to the world, neither as refuge nor as ensemble of purposes. In this word, the world recedes and purposes have ceased, the world is silent. It is no longer beings with their worries, plans and activities, who speak. The fact that beings are silent is expressed in the poetic word,"[20] in the sense that, in the poetic word, no person speaks any more; "nobody speaks, and the person who speaks is nobody, and it seems that the word is a self-utterance."[21]

Thus, poetry is a "powerful universe of words whose relationships, composition and powers are asserted in the sound, figure, and rhythmic

---

[18]OC., p. 851.

[19]Cf. R. DRAGONETTI, *Le sens de l'"oublie" dans l'oeuvre de Mallarmé*, in *Aux frontières du langage poétique* cit., p.148.

[20]M. BLANCHOT, *L'espace littéraire* cit., p. 27.

[21]Ibid.

mobility, within a unified, sovereign, autonomous space."[22] In *poiesis*, in short, where nothing but the nature of words is reflected, man is nullified, and what Sartre has called the "critical destruction" of poetry[23] is finally accomplished.

Rilke moves in the footsteps of Mallarmé's aesthetic. For Rilke the poetic word and the "disappearance" belong "to the depths of the same movement." Orpheus points to the eternal poem that enters "its own disappearance." In him, poetry becomes *relationship with absence*. However, while for the author of *Igitur* "absence remains the force of the negative, that which repels `the reality of things', freeing us from their weight,"[24] for Rilke "absence is also the presence of things, the innerness of being-a-thing in which one finds the desire to fall towards the center in a silent, unmoving, endless fall."[25] If, for the author of the *Duinese Elegies*, to speak is to celebrate, that is, to tell when there is nothing more to tell, in Mallarmé the word annihilates beings and things through its power of erasure and nullification.

Nothingness, revealing *le défaut d'être*, is a *manière d'être*; "Rien n'aura eu que le lieu" is the ontological seal of *Un coup de Dés*. "Rien, cette écume, vierge vers" is the first verse of the *Poésies*. Here nothingness is the extreme space in which the very destiny of poetry is consumed, whereas in Rilke it is

---

[22]Ibid.

[23]J.P. SARTRE, *Préface* to S. MALLARME, *Poésies*, Paris 1952, pp. 5-15.

[24]M. BLANCHOT, *L'espace littéraire* cit. (p. 135).

[25]Ibid.

the boundary line staking out the ground of *poiesis* and defining its horizon of meaning.

4.   In a passage of his *Rodin*, Rilke notes that the great French artist knew how to make works that would live on their own, things that could "stand by themselves," and he adds that all of Rodin's artistic production, distinct as it is from the infinite number of ordinary things, appears unattainable, sacrosanct and detached from Chance and Time; indeed, it belongs to "the silent duration of space and in the order of its great laws."[26] In another passage, Rilke writes: "...It is not movement in general that is in contrast with the essence of sculpture..., but only *unfinished* movement, movement not kept in equilibrium by other movements, a movement which, in short, overflows the precise limits of the sculpted object. The sculpted object resembles those ancient cities shut up within the circle of their walls. The inhabitants did not hold their breath on that account, nor did the gestures of their lives come to a paralyzed halt, but nothing exceeded the limits of the walls. Beyond the walls was nothingness, nobody ventured outside the gates, and no expectation forced a breach towards the outside. "However great the movement of the subject of a sculpture may be, whether it comes from the infinity of space or from the depths of the skies,

---

[26]*Auguste Rodin*, in R.M. RILKE, *Liriche e prose*, (It. trans. V. Errante), Firenze 1961, p. 869.

that movement *must* always return to the sculpted object, so that the circle of solitude in which a work of art passes its days may be closed."[27]

Thus, sculpture (and all the other arts along with it, even those of the word) is a thing, enclosed in its inner rest, absorbed in itself, asking for nothing from without, expecting nothing; it does not seek any reference with the outside, it is blind "to everything which is not inside itself". Its external world is enclosed in itself. Rilke notes that in the human figures sculpted by Rodin there is an "Everything," which is revealed, besides, in the web of relations between the parts of distinct bodies, which "adhere to each other by virtue of an inner necessity and are ordered... in the unitary harmony of an organism."[28] Thus, in the encounter between things, the "new," "something more," is born, which "has no name and does not belong to anybody".

Rodin has subjugated light and conquered space: "Natural things out there, and some objects created by art, famous in origin, which he happened continuously to turn to, questioning them anew. They continued to repeat to him laws and precepts of which they themselves were overflowing, and which he gradually understood more and more. And they permitted him to take a glimpse into a mysterious geometry of space, which revealed to him how the contours of every object must be ordered by the guiding line of certain planes

---

[27]Ibid., p. 878.

[28]Ibid., p. 885.

inclined towards each other, so that the object can really be contained in space and obtain from it the acknowledgement of its full cosmic independence".[29]

Thus, laws, precepts and cosmic independence are the texture of the work-thing, which participates in the cosmos and "stretches itself to infinity." In the work the *Vollendung* is realized or perfection accomplished, which becomes the *immaterial zone* located at the limits of the very strategy of making, in which the work's existence as a work becomes history. And the work's existence as a work is the "essence" of art, the ontological space it conquers in things. This space, however, even if *it signifies itself* in things, has the configuration of a place "with no reason why," a place which is given – we can use a felicitous image of Eckhart's – as a mode without a mode, as being without being.

The artist can accede to the abode of being only when he has succeeded in stepping himself outside his own psychological subjectivity, cutting himself off from the daily world. Rodin was a *worker*, who, by a sort of renunciation of life, managed to penetrate the all; indeed, precisely by virtue of this renunciation, he conquered life: "... the universe ended by coming, docilely, to his tools." It is thus that his work, in *gathering* the universe, transformed into *thing*s, which can stand by themselves and which, distinct from the infinite number of ordinary objects, *appear* as the abode where the concordance of the One with the All is realized and the multiplicity of forms are unified in the horizon of *Allgemeinheit*.

---

[29]Ibid., p. 932.

5.   Rodin "placed" his work in historical time, and, at the same time, gave it a metatemporal dimension. In other words he "placed" it in the space of *poiesis*, which lies at the limits of history. This is the space *intuited* by Hölderlin, who, grasping the character of the poetic individuality in the concordance of *Identität der Begeisterung* and *Vollendung*, considered the site of poetry not as empty individuality but as the limit within which it was possible to rediscover both the "poetry of an infinite divine being" and the poetic I; the site of the *lebendige Anschauung*, the *lebendige Schönheit*, where the *differences* beyond the chaos of time might be reconciled.[30]

Thus with his work Rodin represents in exemplary fashion not only the inseparability of what – one might say with Hölderlin – is in harmonic opposition but also the *living presence* of the absolute in the sensible and, above all, the very destiny of poetic making. Rodin's acting is pure, moved by a sort of *Wille zur Dichtung*, a Promethean tension towards things. But *things* are not mere objectivity, the other than ourselves; they are the very innerness of art.

Let us consider the Victor Hugo monument, which Rodin spent so long a time on. There was a great deal of laborious preparatory work, as attested by the many portraits of the writer; many are the suggestions and impressions "gathered" by Rodin. But then he rejected the single impressions and created a single figure, on which he bestowed the dimension of legend: "As if all of

---

[30]Hölderlin, following the Fichtian *Doctrine of science*, constructs an authentic *Dichtungslehre*, addressed to grasping and fixing the specific property of poetry.

this ultimately could only have been myth and had to return to one of those fantastic sea rocks, in whose mysterious forms primitive peoples saw, sleeping, the enigma of a gesture."[31] Like Hölderlin's Empedocles, who – *born absolutely to be a poet* – knows how to appropriate everything vitally in its totality, Rodin transfigures the world within an order in which the single finds its due place within the *whole*. In fact, Rodin has expressed in his work the relations between things. They establish complicated connections in real life, which cannot be grasped on the plane of abstract conceptual reflection but in the harmony of gestures and meanings that combine continuously in the web of making. This does not consist in the pursuance of an unattainable Beauty but in the capacity to comprehend and unveil the enigma buried beneath things.

The artist, every true artist, does nothing but move towards an *almost practical* activity, which, nevertheless, transcends his own human nature: "All he knows is that there are certain `conditions,' given which, perhaps, Beauty will deign to descend upon things. His task is to learn to know them and acquire the power to produce them."[32] The idea of the Beautiful that descends upon things is a metaphor for the horizon of meanings proper to poetic making, offered as the *total* connection of life (*Zusammenhang des Lebens*). Rilke adds: "...whoever pursues these conditions to the end notices that they never exceed the surface limits and never enter into the heart of the thing. He

---

[31]R.M. RILKE, *Auguste Rodin* cit., p. 906.

[32]Ibid., p. 924.

notices that everything it is possible to create is reduced only to this, to produce a surface enclosed in a certain manner; in no point random; enveloped by the atmosphere in a play of shadows and lights. This surface, and nothing else."[33]

Two salient remarks emerge from Rilke's analysis. First, art appears to be led back to an "almost prosaic reality," to a normal craft. Second, poetic making is nothing but an "intervention" on the surface, and nothing more. All that we call *soul, spirit* or *love* "is reduced" to a faint alteration of lines, a form open to the various modes of sensibility and subjective perception. Form is surface, "infinitely moving and changeable," capable, however, of gathering the totality of the universe. How? Through perennial metamorphotic play, passing along the paths of *techne*, of craft: "...the metamorphosis of any nothingness into the concreteness of life does not spout... directly from great ideas. But from the great ideas, (the artist) must first forge a craft, which is humble and everyday."[34]

In our age, which no longer has "things" or abodes or externals, and in which the internal is amorphous and passes by ineffably, the surface fixes the universe and sets itself as the enigmatic site of poetic making. We might say, with an image from the *Ninth Elegy*: "*Hier* ist des *Säglichen Zeit, hier* seine Heimat". The surface, that is to say, the "form," is to be understood here not only, in the meaning of Aristotle, as the *extreme term*, the *end* and the *essence*

---

[33]Ibid.

[34]Ibid., p. 926.

of the *poiein*,[35] but as a boundary concept (*Grenz-begriff*) located at the threshold of metaphysics.

6.   If, as the formalists say, the form of poetry (taken here as the entire phenomenology of art) is an element *sui generis*, which cannot schematically be reduced to the other elements, *poeticalness* is nothing but a component of a complex structure, "a component which, however, transforms the other elements and along with them determines the character of the whole."[36] Only when *poeticalness* acquires decisive value in a work is it possible to talk of poetry. In other words, the *poetic character* is manifested in a work, when gesture is felt as gesture, "the word as word and not the simple replacement of the named object, nor as the explosion of emotion."[37]

This means that the poetic function, and it alone, organizes and governs the work of art. Furthermore, it makes possible the transformation of things, whether objects or words, into the *other*. "An impartial, careful, exhaustive and complete description of the selection, distribution and reciprocal relations of the diverse morphological classes and syntactic constructions of a given poem surprises...by unexpected, noteworthy symmetries, antisymmetries and balanced structures, by the skilful accumulation of equivalent forms and salient contrasts, finally by the rigid restrictions in the repertory of

---

[35]In particular ARISTOTLE, *Metaphysics*, Book Delta,17.

[36]Cf. R. JAKOBSON, *Poetica e prosa* cit., p. 52.

[37]Ibid., p. 53.

morphological and syntactic constituents used in the poem; the absence of what has been eliminated allows us to follow the masterful play of what has been put to use."[38]

The play has the configuration of a monad but, nevertheless, it can cause the language imposed by tradition "break into flame" or create breaks and openings within the multiple and multivocal *institutions* of art.[39] Consequently, the text, the achieved work in its "poetic function" is offered as a possible realization of a process which "demeure toujours virtuellement présent à l'arrière-plan et constitue comme une troisième dimension..."[40] In this dimension the fate of the work "se joue avec des élans et des épuisements, des bégaiements et des vides, des ruptures et des inachévements..."[41] The work, in short, is given as a complex object, strictly tied to life and, at the same time, far from life.

It is given as *surface*, in the sense that here space "takes you, proceeds with you, goes with you towards everything and crosses everything, large and small. Everything that was is ordered in a different way; it lines up as if there were somebody in command; and the Present is present with great insistence,

---

[38]Ibid., p. 345.

[39]Cf. D. DELAS-J. FILLIOLET, *Linguistique et poétique*, Paris 1973.

[40]L. HAY, in his essay *Le texte n'existe pas. Réflexions sur la critique génétique*, in "Poétique," 62, Paris, avril 1985, p. 158.

[41]Ibid.

almost as if on its knees in prayer..."[42] It is an instant, a line that passes through things, opening onto the unlimited, a line which, on the one hand, closes the making, *techne* or artifices, symmetries and compositive grammars once again, on the other hand, it tends to destroy itself in the movement of losing itself. This line has its only real existence in the gestures it performs, the spaces it is able to save and the wandering through which it leads existences back within their own limits, in this way reaching that empty region where – one might say with Foucault – "being reaches its limit, and where the limit defines being."[43]

To experience the limit means to meet the absence of God and to enter that night of which Bataille speaks, which is not the darkness of thought: "the night has the violence of light. The night is itself the youth and the rapture of thought."[44] But it is not only this. The night is also the boundary-territory where *yesterday* has not yet entirely dissolved and *tomorrow* has not yet arisen. In a place of rare drama in *La Jeune Fille Violaine*, Claudel writes: "...entre l'heure de la lune et celle du soleil,/ Voici la partie de la nuit la plus noire où l'on dort / le plus profondément,/ et l'on ne sait si c'est hier ou demain."[45]

---

[42]R.M. RILKE, *Lettere su Cézanne* cit., p. 27.

[43]Cf. M. FOUCAULT, *Scritti letterari*, (It. trans. C. Milanese, Milano 1984[2d ed], p. 60).

[44]Ibid., p. 71.

[45]These are the words Craon addresses Violaine in P. Claudel's play *La jeune fille Violaine* (deuxième version), in P. CLAUDEL, *Théatre*, tome I (introduction et chronologie par J. Madaule), Paris 1956, p. 573.

INDEX

ALDO TRIONE

Aldo Trione is the distinguished Professor of Aesthetics at the University "Frederico II," Naples, Italy. From 1987 to 1993, he was Dean of Faculty of Art at The Salerno University. Currently, he is a Visiting Professor in several European universities.

Among his works are: *Il significato e il corpo* (Naples, 1973), *Rêverie e immaginario, L'estetica di G. Bachelard* (Naples, 1981), *Encoñación e imaginario* (Madrid, 1983), *Lostinata armonia* (Roma-Bari, 1992), and *Estetica e Novecento* (Roma-Bari, 1996).

PROBLEMS IN CONTEMPORARY PHILOSOPHY